TOSEL®

BASIC

KB158185

ITC International TOSEL Committee

GRAMMAR 2

CONTENTS

TOSEL® Level Chart TOSEL 단계표

COCOON
아이들이 접할 수 있는 공식 인증 시험의 첫 단계로써, 아이들의 부담을 줄이고 즐겁게 흥미를 유발할 수 있도록 컬러풀한 색상과 디자인으로 시험지를 구성하였습니다.

Pre-STARTER
친숙한 주제에 대한 단어, 짧은 대화, 짧은 문장을 사용한 기본적인 문장표현 능력을 측정합니다.

STARTER
흔히 접할 수 있는 주제와 상황과 관련된 주제에 대한 짧은 대화 및 짧은 문장을 이해하고 일상생활 대화에 참여하며 실질적인 영어 기초 의사소통 능력을 측정합니다.

BASIC
개인 정보와 일상 활동, 미래 계획, 과거의 경험에 대해 구어와 문어의 형태로 의사소통을 할 수 있는 능력을 측정합니다.

JUNIOR
일반적인 주제와 상황을 다루는 회화와 짧은 단락, 실용문, 짧은 연설 등을 이해하고 간단한 일상 대화에 참여하는 능력을 측정합니다.

HIGH JUNIOR
넓은 범위의 사회적, 학문적 주제에서 영어를 유창하고 정확하게, 효과적으로 사용할 수 있는 능력 및 중문과 복잡한 문장을 포함한 다양한 문장구조의 사용 능력을 측정합니다.

ADVANCED
대학 및 대학원에서 요구되는 영어능력과 취업 또는 직업근무환경에 필요한 실용영어 능력을 측정합니다.

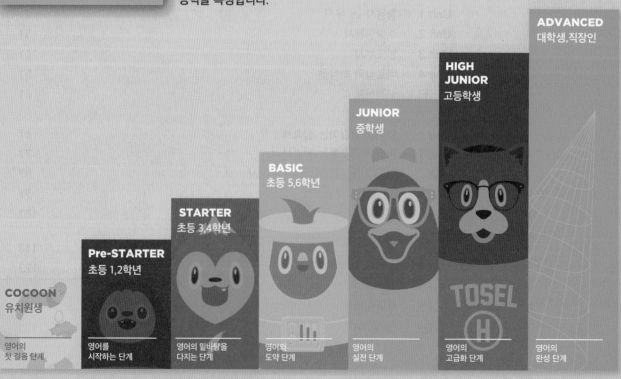

COCOON 유치원생
영어의 첫 걸음 단계

Pre-STARTER 초등 1,2학년
영어를 시작하는 단계

STARTER 초등 3,4학년
영어의 밑바탕을 다지는 단계

BASIC 초등 5,6학년
영어의 도약 단계

JUNIOR 중학생
영어의 실전 단계

HIGH JUNIOR 고등학생
영어의 고급화 단계

ADVANCED 대학생,직장인
영어의 완성 단계

TOSEL
교재 Series

TOSEL LEVEL	Age	Vocabulary Frequency	Readability Score	교과 과정 연계	Grammar	VOCA	Reading	Listening
Cocoon	K5-K7	500	0-1	Who is he? (국어 1단원 1-1)	There is · There are	150	Picking Pumpkins (Phonics Story)	Phonics
Pre-Starter	P1-P2	700		How old are you? (통합교과 1-1)	be + adjective	300	Me & My Family (Reading series Ch.1)	묘사하기
Starter	P3-P4	1000-2000	1-2	Spring, Summer, Fall, Winter (통합교과 3-1)	Simple Present	800	Ask More Questions (Reading Series Ch.1)	날씨/시간 표현
Basic	P5-P6	3000-4000	3-4	Show and Tell (사회 5-1)	Superlative	1700	Culture (Reading Series Ch.3)	상대방 의견 묻고 답하기
Junior	M1-M2	5000-6000	5-6	중 1, 2 과학, 기술가정	to-infinitive	4000	Humans and Animals (Reading Series Ch.1)	정보 묻고 답하기
High Junior	H1-H3			고등학교 - 체육	2nd Conditional	7000	Health (Reading Series Ch.1)	사건 묘사하기

■ TOSEL의 세분화된 레벨은 각 연령에 맞는 어휘와 읽기 지능 및 교과 과정과의 연계가 가능하도록 설계된 교재들로 효과적인 학습 커리큘럼을 제공합니다.

■ TOSEL의 커리큘럼에 따른 학습은

정확한 레벨링 ➔ 레벨에 적합한 학습 ➔ 영어 능력 인증 시험 TOSEL에서의 공신력 있는 평가를 통해

진단 ➔ 학습 ➔ 평가의 선순환 구조를 실현합니다.

About TOSEL®

TOSEL은 각급 학교 교과과정과 연령별 인지단계를 고려하여 단계별 난이도와 문항으로
영어 숙달 정도를 측정하는 영어 사용자 중심의 맞춤식 영어능력인증 시험제도입니다.
평가유형에 따른 개인별 장점과 단점을 파악하고, 개인별 영어학습 방향을 제시하는 성적분석자료를 제공하여
영어능력 종합검진 서비스를 제공함으로써 영어 사용자인 소비자와
영어능력 평가를 토대로 영어교육을 담당하는 교사 및 기관 인사관리자인 공급자를
모두 만족시키는 영어능력인증 평가입니다.

TOSEL은 인지적-학문적 언어 사용의 유창성 (Cognitive-Academic Language Proficiency, CALP)과
기본적-개인적 의사소통능력 (Basic Interpersonal Communication Skill, BICS)을
엄밀히 구분하여 수험자의 언어능력을 가장 친밀하게 평가하는 시험입니다.

대상	목적	용도
유아, 초, 중, 고등학생, 대학생 및 직장인 등 성인	한국인의 영어구사능력 증진과 비영어권 국가의 영어 사용자의 영어구사능력 증진	실질적인 영어구사능력 평가 + 입학전형 및 인재선발 등에 활용 및 직무역량별 인재 배치

연혁

2002.02	국제토셀위원회 창설 (수능출제위원역임 전국대학 영어전공교수진 중심)
2004.09	TOSEL 고려대학교 국제어학원 공동인증시험 실시
2006.04	EBS 한국교육방송공사 주관기관 참여
2006.05	민족사관고등학교 입학전형에 반영
2008.12	고려대학교 편입학시험 TOSEL 유형으로 대체
2009.01	서울시 공무원 근무평정에 TOSEL 점수 가산점 부여
2009.01	전국 대부분 외고, 자사고 입학전형에 TOSEL 반영 (한영외국어고등학교, 한일고등학교, 고양외국어고등학교, 과천외국어고등학교, 김포외국어고등학교, 명지외국어고등학교, 부산국제외국어고등학교, 부일외국어 고등학교, 성남외국어고등학교, 인천외국어고등학교, 전북외국어고등학교, 대전외국어고등학교, 청주외국어고등학교, 강원외국어고등학교, 전남외국어고등학교)
2009.12	청심국제중·고등학교 입학전형 TOSEL 반영
2009.12	한국외국어교육학회, 팬코리아영어교육학회, 한국음성학회, 한국응용언어학회 TOSEL 인증
2010.03	고려대학교, TOSEL 출제기관 및 공동 인증기관으로 참여
2010.07	경찰청 공무원 임용 TOSEL 성적 가산점 부여
2014.04	전국 200개 초등학교 단체 응시 실시
2017.03	중앙일보 주관기관 참여
2018.11	관공서, 대기업 등 100여 개 기관에서 TOSEL 반영
2019.06	미얀마 TOSEL 도입 발족식 베트남 TOSEL 도입 협약식
2019.11	2020학년도 고려대학교 편입학전형 반영
2020.04	국토교통부 국가자격시험 TOSEL 반영
2021.07	소방청 간부후보생 선발시험 TOSEL 반영

About TOSEL

What's TOSEL?

"Test of Skills in the English Language"

TOSEL은 비영어권 국가의 영어 사용자를 대상으로 영어구사능력을 측정하여
그 결과를 공식 인증하는 영어능력인증 시험제도입니다.

영어 사용자 중심의 맞춤식 영어능력 인증 시험제도

맞춤식 평가

**획일적인 평가에서
세분화된 평가로의 전환**

TOSEL은 응시자의 연령별
인지단계에 따라 별도의 문항과 난이도를
적용하여 평가함으로써 평가의
목적과 용도에 적합한 평가 시스템을
구축하였습니다.

공정성과 신뢰성 확보

국제토셀위원회의 역할

TOSEL은 고려대학교가 출제 및 인증기관
으로 참여하였고 대학입학수학능력시험 출
제위원 교수들이
중심이 된 국제토셀위원회가 주관하여
사회적 공정성과 신뢰성을 확보한
평가 제도입니다.

수입대체 효과

외화유출 차단 및 국위선양

TOSEL은 해외시험응시로 인한 외화의 유
출을 막는 수입대체의 효과를 기대할 수 있
습니다. TOSEL의 문항과 시험제도는 비영
어권 국가에 수출하여 국위선양에
기여하고 있습니다.

Why TOSEL®

왜 TOSEL인가

01 학교 시험 폐지

일선 학교에서 중간, 기말고사 폐지로 인해 객관적인 영어 평가 제도의 부재가 우려됩니다. 그러나 전국단위로 연간 4번 시행되는 TOSEL 평가시험을 통해 학생들은 정확한 역량과 체계적인 학습방향을 꾸준히 진단받을 수 있습니다.

02 연령별/단계별 대비로 영어학습 점검

TOSEL은 응시자의 연령별 인지단계 및 영어 학습 단계에 따라 총 7단계로 구성되었습니다. 각 단계에 알맞은 문항유형과 난이도를 적용해 모든 연령 및 학습 과정에 맞추어 가장 효율적으로 영어실력을 평가할 수 있도록 개발된 영어시험입니다.

03 학교내신성적 향상

TOSEL은 학년별 교과과정과 연계하여 학교에서 배우는 내용을 학습하고 평가할 수 있도록 문항 및 주제를 구성하여 내신영어 향상을 위한 최적의 솔루션을 제공합니다.

04 수능대비 직결

유아, 초, 중등시절 어렵지 않고 즐겁게 학습해 온 영어이지만, 수능시험준비를 위해 접하는 영어의 문항 및 유형 난이도에 주춤하게 됩니다. 이를 대비하기 위해 TOSEL은 유아부터 성인까지 점진적인 학습을 통해 수능대비를 자연적으로 해나갈 수 있습니다.

05 진학과 취업에 대비한 필수 스펙관리

개인별 '학업성취기록부' 발급을 통해 영어학업성취이력을 꾸준히 기록한 영어학습 포트폴리오를 제공하여 영어학습 이력을 관리할 수 있습니다.

06 자기소개서에 토셀 기재

개별적인 진로 적성 Report를 제공하여 진로를 파악하고 자기소개서 작성시 적극적으로 활용할 수 있는 객관적인 자료를 제공합니다.

07 영어학습 동기부여

시험실시 후 응시자 모두에게 수여되는 인증서는 영어학습에 대한 자신감과 성취감을 고취시키고 동기를 부여합니다.

08 AI 분석 영어학습 솔루션

국내외 15,000여 개 학교·학원 단체 응시인원 중 엄선한 100만 명 이상의 실제 TOSEL 성적 데이터를 기반으로 영어인증시험 제도 중 세계 최초로 인공지능이 분석한 개인별 AI 정밀 진단 성적표를 제공합니다. 최첨단 AI 정밀진단 성적표는 최적의 영어 학습 솔루션을 제시하여 영어 학습에 소요되는 시간과 노력을 획기적으로 절감해줍니다.

09 명예의 전당, 우수협력기관 지정

우수교육기관은 'TOSEL 우수 협력 기관'에 지정되고, 각 시/도별, 최고득점자를 명예의 전당에 등재합니다.

Evaluation ──────── 평가

평가의 기본원칙

TOSEL은 PBT(Paper Based Test)를 통하여 간접평가와 직접평가를 모두 시행합니다.

TOSEL은 언어의 네 가지 요소인 **읽기, 듣기, 말하기, 쓰기 영역을 모두 평가합니다.**

문자언어
- 읽기능력
- 쓰기능력

음성언어
- 듣기능력
- 말하기능력

대한민국 대표 영어능력 인증 시험제도

TOSEL®

Reading 읽기	모든 레벨의 읽기 영역은 직접 평가 방식으로 측정합니다.
Listening 듣기	모든 레벨의 듣기 영역은 직접 평가 방식으로 측정합니다.
Writing 쓰기	모든 레벨의 쓰기 영역은 간접 평가 방식으로 측정합니다.
Speaking 말하기	모든 레벨의 말하기 영역은 간접 평가 방식으로 측정합니다.

TOSEL은 연령별 인지단계를 고려하여 **아래와 같이 7단계로 나누어 평가합니다.**

1 단계	**TOSEL**® COCOON	5~7세의 미취학 아동
2 단계	**TOSEL**® Pre-STARTER	초등학교 1~2학년
3 단계	**TOSEL**® STARTER	초등학교 3~4학년
4 단계	**TOSEL**® BASIC	초등학교 5~6학년
5 단계	**TOSEL**® JUNIOR	중학생
6 단계	**TOSEL**® HIGH JUNIOR	고등학생
7 단계	**TOSEL**® ADVANCED	대학생 및 성인

Grade Report

성적표 및 인증서

개인 AI 정밀진단 성적표

십 수년간 전국단위 정기시험으로 축적된 빅데이터를 교육공학적으로 분석 · 활용하여 산출한 개인별 성적자료

정확한 영어능력진단 / 섹션별 · 파트별 영어능력 및 균형 진단 / 명예의 전당 등재 여부 / 온라인 최적화된 개인별 상세 성적자료를 위한 QR코드 / 응시지역, 동일학년, 전국에서의 학생의 위치

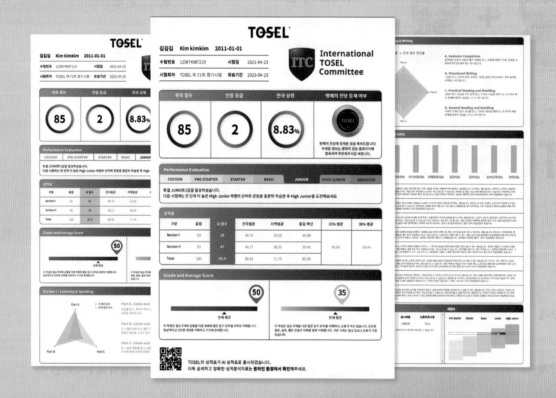

단체 및 기관 응시자 AI 통계 분석 자료

십 수년간 전국단위 정기시험으로 **축적된 빅데이터를**
교육공학적으로 분석 · 활용하여 산출한 응시자 통계 분석 자료

- 단체 내 레벨별 평균성적추이, LR평균 점수, 표준편차 파악
- 타 지역 내 다른 단체와의 점수 종합 비교 / 단체 내 레벨별
  학생분포 파악
- 동일 지역 내 다른 단체 레벨별 응시자의 평균 나이 비교
- 동일 지역 내 다른 단체 명예의 전당 등재 인원 수 비교
- 동일 지역 내 다른 단체 최고점자의 최고 점수 비교
- 동일 지역 내 다른 응시자들의 수 비교

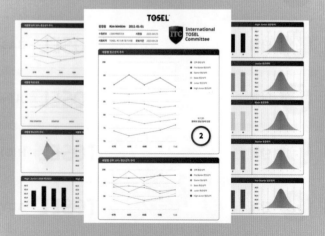

'토셀 명예의 전당' 등재

특별시, 광역시, 도 별 **1등 선발**
(7개시 9개도 **1등 선발**)

*홈페이지 로그인 – 시험결과 – 명예의 전당에서
 해당자 등재 증명서 출력 가능

'학업성취기록부'에 토셀 인증등급 기재

개인별 **'학업성취기록부'** 평생 발급
진학과 취업을 대비한 **필수 스펙관리**

인증서

대한민국 초,중,고등학생의 영어숙달능력 평가 결과 공식인증

고려대학교 인증획득 (2010. 03)　팬코리아영어교육학회 인증획득 (2009. 10)　한국응용언어학회 인증획득 (2009. 11)

한국외국어교육학회 인증획득 (2009. 12)　한국음성학회 인증획득 (2009. 12)

Grammar Series ——— 특장점

TOSEL 시험을 기준으로 빈출 지표를 활용한 문법 선정 및 예문과 문제 구성

TOSEL 시험 활용

■ 실제 TOSEL 시험에 출제된 빈출 문항을 기준으로 단계별 학습을 위한 문법 선정

■ 실제 TOSEL 시험에 활용된 문장을 사용하여 예문과 문제를 구성

■ 문법 학습 이외에 TOSEL 기출 문제 풀이를 통해서 TOSEL 및 실전 영어 시험 대비 학습

세분화된 레벨링

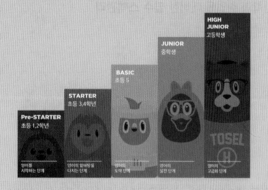

20년 간 대한민국 영어 평가 기관으로서

연간 4회 전국적으로 실시되는 정기시험에서

축적된 성적 데이터를 기반으로

정확하고 세분화된 레벨링을 통한

영어 학습 콘텐츠 개발

언어의 4대 영역 균형 학습 + 평가

1   TOSEL 평가: 학생의 영어 능력을 정확하게 평가

2   결과 분석 및 진단: 시험 점수와 결과를 분석하여 학생의 강점, 취약점, 학습자 특성 등을 객관적으로 진단

3   학습 방향 제시: 객관적 진단 데이터를 기반으로 학습자 특성에 맞는 학습 방향 제시 및 목표 설정

4   학습: 제시된 방향과 목표에 따라 학생에게 적합한 문법 학습법 소개 및 영어의 체계와 구조 이해

5   학습 목표 달성: 학습 후 다시 평가를 통해 목표 달성 여부 확인 및 성장을 위한 다음 학습 목표 설정

Grammar Series ——— Level

TOSEL의 Grammar Series는 레벨에 맞게 단계적으로
문법을 학습할 수 있도록 구성되어 있습니다.

| Pre-Starter | Starter | Basic | Junior | High Junior |

- 그림을 활용하여 문법에 대한 이해도 향상
- 다양한 활동을 통해 문법 반복 학습 유도
- TOSEL 기출 문제 연습을 통한 실전 대비

- TOSEL 기출의 빈도수를 활용한 문법 선정으로 효율적 학습
- 실제 TOSEL 지문의 예문을 활용한 실용적 학습 제공
- TOSEL 기출 문제 연습을 통한 실전 대비

최신 수능 출제
문법을 포함하여
수능 대비 가능

1시간 학습 Guideline

01 Unit Intro
2분

■ 초등 교육과정에서 익혀야 하는 문법과 단어를 중심으로 단원의 문법에 대해 미리 생각해보기

02 개념
15분

■ 문법 개념을 익히고 예문을 통해 문법이 어떻게 적용되는지 익히기

05 Sentence Completion
10분

■ Unit에서 배운 문법을 활용하여 문제 해결하기

■ 틀린 문제에 대해서는 해당 Unit에서 복습하도록 지도하기

06 Writing Activity
3분

■ 빈도수가 높은 주요 단어 위주로 writing activity를 추가하여 쓰기 학습 지도

■ 단어를 소리 내어 읽으며, 점선을 따라 스펠링을 쓰도록 지도하기

03 Activity 1 / Activity 2

5분

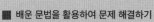

■ 배운 문법을 활용하여 문제 해결하기

■ 연결하기, OX 문제, 빈칸 채우기 등
다양한 방법으로 문법 적용하기

04 Exercise 1 / Exercise 2

5분

■ 다양한 Exercise 활동을 하며 혼동하기 쉬운
문법 학습

07  Unit Review

10분

■ 빈칸을 채우는 형태로 구성하여 수업 시간 후
복습에 용이하게 구성

■ 배운 문법을 직접 활용하여 수업 시간 후
복습에 용이하게 구성

08 TOSEL 실전문제

10분

■ 실제 TOSEL 기출 문제를 통한 실전 대비 학습

■ 실제 시험 시간과 유사하게 풀이할 수 있도록 지도하기

■ 틀린 문제에 대해서는 해당 단원에서 복습하도록 지도하기

PreStarter/Starter/Basic ── Syllabus

PreStarter		Basic		2015 개정 초등 영어 언어형식
Chapter	Unit	Chapter	Unit	
I. 명사: 명사는 이름이야	1 셀 수 있는 명사	I. 명사	1 셀 수 있는 명사 앞에 붙는 관사 the/a/an	**A** boy/The **boy**/The (two) boys ran in the park. **The** store is closed.
	2 셀 수 있는 명사 앞에 붙는 관사 a/an		2 셀 수 없는 명사를 측정하는 단위	**Water** is very important for life. **Kate** is from **London**.
	3 셀 수 없는 명사		3 규칙 복수명사	
	4 명사의 복수형		4 불규칙 복수명사	The **two boys** ran in the park.
II. 대명사: 명사를 대신하는 대명사	1 주격 대명사	II. 대명사	1 단수대명사의 격	**She** is a teacher, and **he**'s a scientist. I like **your** glasses. What about **mine**?
	2 소유격 대명사		2 복수대명사의 격	**They**'re really delicious. **We** are very glad to hear from him.
	3 목적격 대명사		3 1, 2인칭 대명사의 활용	**I** like math, but Susan doesn't like **it**. He will help **you**.
	4 지시대명사		4 3인칭 대명사의 활용	Which do you like better, **this** or **that**? **These** are apples, and **those** are tomatoes. **That** dog is smart. **These/Those** books are really large.
III. 형용사: 명사&대명사를 꾸미는 형용사	1 형용사의 명사수식	III. 동사	1 동사의 기본시제	He **walks** to school every day. We **played** soccer yesterday. She **is going to** visit her grandparents next week. He **is sleeping** now. I **will visit** America next year.
	2 형용사의 대명사수식		2 동사의 불규칙 과거형	
	3 숫자와 시간		3 헷갈리기 쉬운 동사	**It's half past four.** **What time** is it? I **don't** like snakes. We **didn't** enjoy the movie very much.
	4 지시형용사		4 조동사	She **can** play the violin. Tom **won't** be at the meeting tomorrow. I **will** visit America next year. You **may** leave now.

Junior Syllabus

High Junior Syllabus

High Junior		2015 개정 중등 영어 언어형식
Chapter	**Unit**	
I. 문장의 형성	1 8품사와 문장 성분	**The audience** is/are enjoying the show. I'd like to **write a diary**, but I'm too busy to do so.
	2 문장의 형식	He**'s being** very rude. We **are hoping** you will be with us.
	3 문장의 배열	I think **(that)** he is a good actor. **Although/Though** it was cold, I went swimming.
	4 문장의 강조	The weather was **so** nice **that** we went hiking. **It was** Justin **who/that** told me the truth.
II 부정사와 동명사	1 원형부정사	You shouldn't **let** him **go** there again. I **heard** the children **sing/singing**.
	2 to부정사	He seemed **to have been ill (for some time)**.
	3 동명사	Bill promised Jane **to work out with her**. I remembered **John/John's coming** late for class.
	4 to부정사와 동명사구	It goes without **saying that time is money**. There is no use **crying over the spilt milk**.
III. 분사	1 현재분사	At the station I met a lady **carrying a large umbrella**. **With the night coming**, stars began to shine in the sky.
	2 과거분사	Wallets **found on the street** must be reported to the police.
	3 분사구문	**Walking along the street,** I met an old friend. **Having seen that movie before,** I wanted to see it again.
	4 독립분사구문	**Joshua returning home,** the puppy ran toward him. **Frankly speaking,** I failed the test.
IV. 수동태	1 수동태의 형성	The building **was built** in 1880. I **was made** to clean the room.
	2 수동태와 능동태의 전환	Nolan **was seen** to enter the building. The monkey **has been raised** by human parents for years.
	3 수동태와 전치사의 사용	Cooper **will be invited** to today's meeting. The information superhighway **will have been introduced** to everyone by 2015.
	4 주의해야 할 수동태 용법	
V. 관계대명사와 관계부사	1 관계대명사의 사용	The girl **who is playing the piano** is called Ann. This is the book **(that) I bought yesterday**.
	2 관계대명사와 선행사	Please tell me **what happened**.
	3 관계대명사의 생략	This is **why** we have to study English grammar.
	4 관계부사	The town **in which I was born** is very small. That's just **how he talks**, always serious about his work.
VI. 가정법	1 가정법 현재와 과거	**If it were not for you, I would** be lonely.
	2 가정법 과거완료	**Had** I had enough money, I **would have bought** a cell phone. **Without/But for** your advice, I **would have** failed.
	3 혼합가정법	**I wish I had learned** swimming last summer. He acts **as if he had been** there.
	4 특수가정법	I'd **rather** we **had** dinner now. **Provided that/As long as** they had plenty to eat, the crew **seemed** to be happy.

CHAPTER 04

IV. 형용사와 부사

UNIT 01

형용사 vs. 부사

형용사	주로 명사를 수식하고, 상태나 성질을 나타냄
부사	주로 동사나 문장 전체를 수식하고, '-ly'로 끝나는 형태임

quickly	빠르게	marvelous	기막히게 좋은
memorize	암기하다	final	마지막의
swallow	삼키다	quiet	조용한
trust	믿다, 신뢰하다	silly	어리석은
small	작은	fortunately	다행스럽게도

UNIT 1 형용사 vs 부사

❶ 형용사의 부사로의 전환

형용사에 '-ly'가 붙는 경우

He can **quick**ly memorize the words.   '형용사 + -ly'

The snake **easi**ly swallowed it.   '-y로 끝나는 형용사 + ly'

We **tru**ly trust you.   '-le[ue]로 끝나는 형용사 + ly'

I **whol**ly agree with them.   예외

형용사와 부사의 형태가 같은 경우

❶ 형용사	❷ 부사
Her job is hard work, but the pay is good.	We worked hard.
The project is still in early stage.	Tom always gets up early.
I am a fast learner.	He runs fast.
I feel well today.	Our project is doing well.

❷ 형용사와 부사의 쓰임 비교

형용사의 쓰임

❶ 명사 수식

He lives in a small town.

❷ 대명사 수식

I need something hot to drink.

❸ 주어 보충 설명

She is marvelous.

부사의 쓰임

① **형용사 수식**

You look so young.

② **동사 수식**

He spoke loudly at the party.

③ **부사 수식**

Kim speaks English very well.

④ **문장 전체 수식**

Fortunately, I could go to the museum.

Activity 1

다음 형용사의 알맞은 부사형 단어에 연결해보세요.

quick   ●   ●   hard

easy   ●   ●   quickly

true   ●   ●   easily

hard   ●   ●   truly

Activity 2

다음 중 줄마다 품사가 다른 것을 골라 색칠하세요.

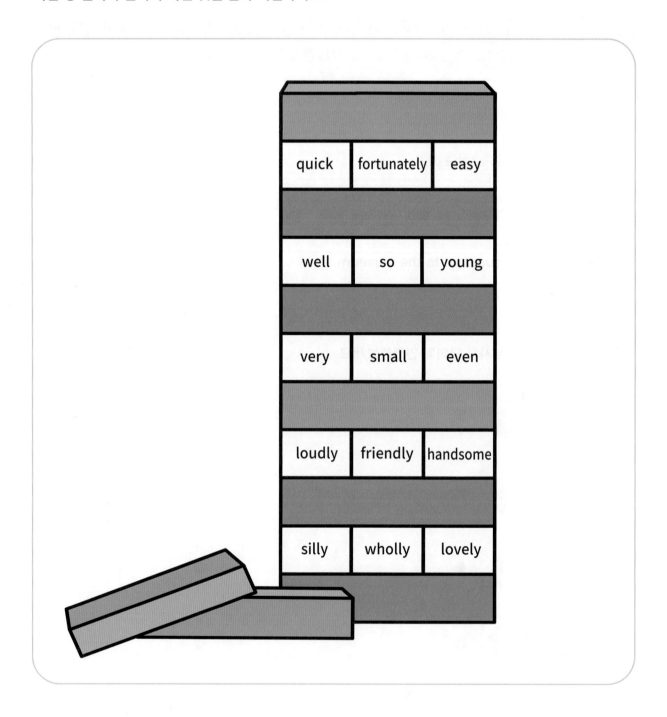

Exercise 1

알맞은 단어를 골라 문장을 완성하세요.

❶ He trusts other people   **easy / easily** .

❷ They can eat   **fast / fastly** .

❸ It is a   **huge / hugely**   ice cream.

❹ The man is   **strong so / so strong** .

❺ We need   **something small / small something** .

Exercise 2

보기의 단어를 적절한 형태로 활용하여, 빈칸에 알맞은 단어를 쓰세요.

| 보기 | busy | correct | quick | hard | early |

❶ We met _____ in the morning.
우리는 아침 일찍 만났다.

❷ He is quite _____ .
그는 꽤 바쁘다.

❸ You should write _____ .
너는 올바르게 써야한다.

❹ The soldiers are running _____ .
군인들이 빠르게 달리는 중이다.

❺ It is _____ to understand.
그것은 이해하기 어렵다.

✏️ Sentence Completion

1 A: The movie was ░░░░░░ touching.

  B: I think so too.

(A) true

(B) truly

(C) trues

(D) trued

2 A: She is ░░░░░░ to cry.

  B: What's the matter?

(A) like

(B) likes

(C) liked

(D) likely

3 A: ░░░░░░ , the prince killed the monster.

  B: He did a great job.

(A) Final

(B) Finals

(C) Finally

(D) Finaling

4 A: The wolves are coming ░░░░░░ .

  B: I'm afraid of them.

(A) slow

(B) slows

(C) slowly

(D) slowing

5 A: We should read a book ░░░░░░ .

  B: It's so boring.

(A) quiet

(B) quietly

(C) quieted

(D) quieting

6 A: The teacher kicked a ball _____.

B: Then, let's play soccer.

(A) high

(B) higher

(C) height

(D) heighten

9 A: The neighbor's dog barks

_____.

B: It's too noisy.

(A) loud

(B) loudly

(C) louded

(D) louding

7 A: How was the exam?

B: The exam was so _____.

(A) hard

(B) hardly

(C) hardship

(D) hardness

10 A: Why does she get up early?

B: Jin has to go to work very

_____.

(A) earl

(B) early

(C) earlier

(D) earled

8 A: She makes them very _____

and fun.

B: She is good at mathematics.

(A) ease

(B) easy

(C) easily

(D) easing

1 **quickly**

빠르게

quickly

2 **memorize**

암기하다

memorize

3 **swallow**

삼키다

swallow

4 **trust**

믿다, 신뢰하다

trust

5 **small**

작은

small

6 marvelous

기막히게 좋은

7 final

마지막의

8 quiet

조용한

9 silly

어리석은

10 fortunately

다행스럽게도

Unit Review

배운 내용 스스로 정리해보기

❶ 형용사의 부사로의 전환

예시문장 써보기

① complete을 부사로 전환

➔ _____

② hard를 부사로 전환

➔ _____

❷ 형용사와 부사의 쓰임 비교

형용사는 ❶   , ❷   를 수식하고 ❸   (을)를 보충 설명한다.
그리고, 부사는 ❹   , ❺   , ❻   , ❼   를 수식한다.

예시문장 써보기

① 형용사(short)의 명사 수식

➔ _____

② 부사(so)의 형용사 수식

➔ _____

③ 부사(closely)의 동사 수식

➔ _____

UNIT 02

수량형용사

셀 수 있는 명사와 쓰는 수량형용사	셀 수 없는 명사와 쓰는 수량형용사
many	much
a lot of, lots of	
a great[good] number of	a great[good] deal of
a few	a little

many	많은	little	작은
much	많은	applicant	지원자
bookstore	서점	error	오류
interview	인터뷰	advice	조언
few	적은	newspaper	신문

UNIT ② 수량형용사

수나 양을 나타내는 형용사를 수량형용사라고 한다. 수량형용사는 꾸밈을 받는 명사가 셀 수 있는 명사인지 셀 수 없는 명사인지 여부와 수량형용사의 의미에 따라 그 쓰임이 달라진다.

❶ many vs. much 뜻 : 많은

many - 셀 수 있는 명사

My mom baked many cookies in the morning.

Tina has many friends in her class.

They bought many books at the bookstore.

much - 셀 수 없는 명사

There is much money in his wallet.

We had much snow two years ago.

She has much energy now.

❷ a lot of / lots of 뜻 : 많은

셀 수 있는 명사와 셀 수 없는 명사도 함께 쓰일 수 있다. 두 경우 모두 명사에 동사의 수일치를 시켜줘야 한다.

셀 수 있는 명사

There were a lot of[lots of] errors in your writing.

A lot of[lots of] audiences are watching the show.

Lots of[A lot of] interviewers interview the interviewees.

셀 수 없는 명사

There is a lot of[lots of] water in the glass.

There isn't a lot of[lots of] time.

There is lots of[a lot of] information.

❸ many, much와 바꿔 쓸 수 있는 표현

> **many와 바꿔쓸 수 있는 표현**
>
> There are a great[good] number of <u>birds</u> in the park.
>
> We read not a few <u>newspapers</u>.
>
> **much와 바꿔쓸 수 있는 표현**
>
> She needs a good[great] deal of <u>advice</u>.
>
> I need not a little <u>salt</u>.

Activity 1

다음 수량형용사와 적절한 명사에 연결해보세요.

| many | ● | | ● | books |

| | | | ● | money |

| | | | ● | dolls |

| much | ● | | ● | coffee |

Activity 2

주어진 명사 사다리를 타고 내려와서 이와 맞는 적절한 수량 형용사를 작성하세요.

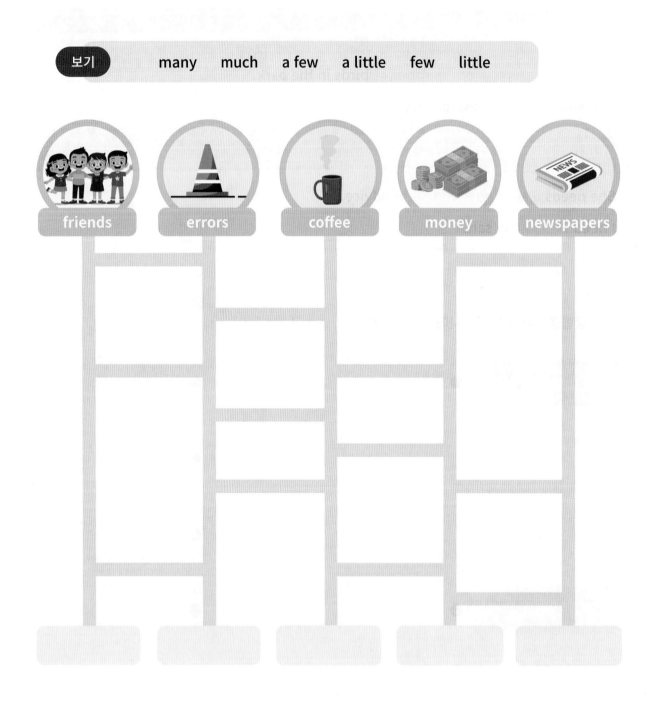

보기   many   much   a few   a little   few   little

friends   errors   coffee   money   newspapers

Exercise 1

알맞은 단어를 골라 문장을 완성하세요.

❶ There are **many / much** people in the park.

❷ We do not have **many / much** time.

❸ You can go to a lot of **bookstore / bookstores** in the city.

❹ I found **a few / a little** errors.

❺ He needs **many / lots of** information.

Exercise 2

보기의 단어를 적절한 형태로 활용하여, 빈칸에 알맞은 단어를 쓰세요.

보기   many   much   lots of   a great deal of   a few

❶ I got _____ advice from you.
나는 너한테 많은 조언을 받았다.

❷ She made _____ friends in the club.
그녀는 동아리에서 많은 친구들을 사귀었다.

❸ You can see _____ furniture at the store.
너는 매장에서 많은 가구들을 볼 수 있다.

❹ The parcel came _____ days ago.
그 소포는 며칠 전에 왔다.

❺ There is so _____ news about the issue.
그 사안에 대한 너무나도 많은 뉴스가 있다.

Sentence Completion

1. A: There are [_____] tigers in the cage.
   B: I would like to see them.

   (A) little
   (B) many
   (C) much
   (D) a little

2. A: Do not drink too [_____] water before running.
   B: Thanks for your advice.

   (A) few
   (B) many
   (C) much
   (D) a few

3. A: I need lots of [_____].
   B: Go to a print shop.

   (A) paper
   (B) papers
   (C) many paper
   (D) much paper

4. A: We have [_____] salt.
   B: Ok, I'll buy it.

   (A) few
   (B) little
   (C) a few
   (D) a little

5. A: You will face [_____] problems.
   B: Don't worry.

   (A) few
   (B) little
   (C) much
   (D) lots of

6 A: There are _____ applicants in this recruitment.

B: It will be hard to pass.

(A) few

(B) much

(C) a little

(D) a number of

9 A: There are only a _____ tomatoes.

B: I'll buy it before dinner.

(A) few

(B) little

(C) much

(D) many

7 A: How far is it from the city?

B: It will take _____ time to go.

(A) few

(B) little

(C) much

(D) many

10 A: _____ of people are waiting for the concert.

B: I can't wait to see the concert.

(A) Lots

(B) Few

(C) Many

(D) Much

8 A: There are _____ countries in Europe.

B: Yes, they also have a long history.

(A) few

(B) little

(C) much

(D) many

1 many
많은

2 much
많은

3 bookstore
서점

4 interview
인터뷰

5 few
적은

6　**little**
　　작은

little

7　**applicant**
　　지원자

applicant

8　**error**
　　오류

error

9　**advice**
　　조언

advice

10　**newspaper**
　　신문

newspaper

Unit Review

배운 내용 스스로 정리해보기

❶ many vs. much

many와 much의 뜻은 '많은'으로 같지만, ❶ [   ] (은)는 셀 수 있는 명사와 함께 쓰이고
❷ [   ] (은)는 셀 수 없는 명사와 함께 쓰인다.

예시문장 써보기

❶ many ➔ _____

❷ much ➔ _____

❷ a lot of/lots of

a lot of와 lots of의 뜻은 '많은'으로 같으며 두 수량형용사 모두 ❶ [   ] 명사와
❷ [   ] 명사도 함께 쓰일 수 있다. 두 경우 모두 ❸ [   ] 에 동사의 수일치를
시켜줘야 한다.

예시문장 써보기

❶ 셀 수 있는 명사와 함께 쓰이는 a lot of

➔ _____

❷ 셀 수 없는 명사와 함께 쓰이는 a lot of

➔ _____

❸ many, much와 바꿔쓸 수 있는 표현

예시문장 써보기

❶ many와 바꿔쓸 수 있는 표현

➔ _____

❷ much와 바꿔쓸 수 있는 표현

➔ _____

UNIT 03

빈도부사

100%		Always	
90%		Usually	
80%		Frequently	
70%		Often	
50%		Sometimes	
30%		Occasionally	
10%		Seldom	
5%		Rarely	
0%		Never	

always	항상	never	전혀 ~아니다
usually	주로	rarely	거의 ~않다
often	자주	passenger	승객
sometimes	때때로	diamond	다이아몬드
seldom	거의 ~않다	solve	해결하다

횟수를 나타내는 **부사**를 빈도부사라고 한다.

❶ 빈도부사의 종류

always 항상[언제나]	She always tries to solve a difficult problem. He always sings a song on the way home.
usually 보통	He usually spends time with his family on weekends. She usually reads books at night.
often 종종	Planes often arrive late. We often meet at the cafe.
sometimes 가끔	She sometimes wears her diamond ring. I sometimes go climbing with my friends.
seldom [rarely, hardly] 좀처럼[거의] ...않다	The passengers seldom[rarely, hardly] fasten their seat belts. Gary seldom[rarely, hardly] reads newspapers.
never 결코 ...않다	I will never be late tomorrow. She never tells a lie.

❷ 빈도부사의 위치

빈도부사의 위치는 **be동사나 조동사의 뒤, 일반동사의 앞**에 위치한다.

---

① be동사의 뒤

Sarah is always kind to everyone.

Cathy is never late for the class.

② 조동사의 뒤, 일반동사의 앞

He may sometimes get up early.

I can hardly run fast.

③ 일반동사의 앞

My family usually eats sandwiches for breakfast.

He often drinks a cup of coffee in the morning.

Activity 1

다음 빈도부사와 적절한 우리말 설명에 연결해보세요.

always	●	●	결코 ~ 않다
sometimes	●	●	좀처럼 ~ 않다
never	●	●	가끔
usually	●	●	보통
seldom	●	●	항상

Activity 2

다음 퍼즐에서 빈도부사를 찾으세요. (5개)

A	N	H	T	A	L	W	D
O	L	P	O	F	T	E	N
S	U	W	C	P	L	Q	A
L	N	H	A	R	D	L	Y
B	E	V	E	Y	O	C	W
A	V	T	C	H	S	M	T
S	E	L	D	O	M	S	A
C	R	C	O	F	T	Y	S

Exercise 1

알맞은 단어를 골라 문장을 완성하세요.

❶ He **always got up / got up always** early.

❷ She **skips usually / usually skips** dinner.

❸ The train **is often / often is** delayed.

❹ He **can hardly / hardly can** run fast.

❺ The diamond **rarely is / is rarely** found.

Exercise 2

보기의 단어를 적절한 형태로 활용하여, 빈칸에 알맞은 단어를 쓰세요.

| 보기 | always   often   usually   sometimes   never |

❶ You should _____ go in there.
너는 절대로 그곳에 들어가면 안된다.

❷ They _____ bite me.
그들은 항상 나를 깨문다.

❸ The leopard _____ hunts at night.
표범은 보통 밤에 사냥한다.

❹ He _____ goes there.
그는 때때로 거기에 간다.

❺ She _____ smiles in front of them.
그녀는 그들 앞에서 자주 미소를 짓는다

Sentence Completion

1 A: What is your hobby?

B: I ⬚⬚⬚⬚⬚⬚ go fishing.

(A) often

(B) never

(C) rarely

(D) seldom

2 A: He ⬚⬚⬚⬚⬚⬚ always kind to other people.

B: He is a good friend.

(A) is

(B) do

(C) does

(D) shows

3 A: Tigers rarely ⬚⬚⬚⬚⬚⬚ plants.

B: They are carnivores.

(A) is

(B) eat

(C) are

(D) can

4 A: Travelers usually ⬚⬚⬚⬚⬚⬚ to the tower.

B: Why don't we go there, too?

(A) is

(B) go

(C) are

(D) goes

5 A: He ⬚⬚⬚⬚⬚⬚ always run fast.

B: He is an athlete.

(A) is

(B) do

(C) are

(D) can

6 A: She _____ locked the door.
B: What is in it?

(A) never
(B) rarely
(C) hardly
(D) always

9 A: If there is a fire, you should _____ go in there.
B: What's the reason?

(A) never
(B) often
(C) always
(D) usually

7 A: He _____ drinks coffee.
B: He doesn't like it.

(A) often
(B) rarely
(C) always
(D) usually

10 A: He _____ looks energetic.
B: I feel good whenever I see him.

(A) never
(B) rarely
(C) always
(D) seldom

8 A: He _____ takes his dictionary.
B: He doesn't use other dictionaries.

(A) never
(B) rarely
(C) seldom
(D) usually

1 always
항상

2 usually
주로

3 often
자주

4 sometimes
때때로

5 seldom
거의 ~않다

6   never
전혀 ~아니다

7   rarely
거의 ~않다

8   passenger
승객

9   diamond
다이아몬드

10   solve
해결하다

 **Unit Review**

배운 내용 스스로 정리해보기

❶ 빈도부사의 종류

빈도부사의 종류로는 ❶ _____, ❷ _____, ❸ _____, ❹ _____, ❺ _____, ❻ _____, 등이 있다

예시문장 써보기

❶ always ➜ _____

❷ usually ➜ _____

❸ often ➜ _____

❷ 빈도부사의 위치

빈도부사의 위치는 ❶ _____ (이)나 ❷ _____ 의 뒤, ❸ _____ 의 앞에 위치한다.

예시문장 써보기

❶ be동사의 뒤 ➜ _____

❷ 조동사의 뒤 ➜ _____

❸ 일반동사의 앞 ➜ _____

UNIT 04

비교급과 최상급

비교급		more	-er	than
최상급	the	most	-est	

more	더 많은 수[양]	important	중요한
most	최대의	attractive	매력적인
interest	관심, 흥미	cheap	싼
large	큰	useful	유용한
worse	더 나쁜	difficult	어려운

UNIT ④ 비교급과 최상급

❶ 비교급

두 가지를 비교하는 데 사용되며 '형용사/부사의 원급 + -er' 또는 'more + 원급'의 형태로 쓰인다. 비교급의 비교 표현은 '비교급 + than…'의 형태를 사용한다.

비교급

① **형용사 / 부사의 원급 + -er** (1, 2음절 형용사)

taller   cheaper   wiser

② **more + 원급** (2, 3음절 이상의 형용사)

more famous   more difficult   more attractive

비교급의 비교 표현

Andy is taller than Hugo.   원급 + -er

Owen is wiser than Thomas.   e로 끝나는 단어 + -r

Summer is hotter than spring.   단모음 + 단자음'으로 끝나는 단어 + 마지막 자음 한 개 더 쓰고 -er

Peter is happier than Robert.   자음 + y'로 끝나는 단어 + y를 i로 고치고 -er

You are more famous than me.   more + -ful, -less, -ous, -ive, -ing으로 끝나는 2음절 단어

This one is more difficult than that one.   more + 3음절 이상의 단어

❷ 최상급

세 가지 이상을 비교하는 데 쓰이며 '형용사 / 부사의 원급 + -est' 또는 'most + 원급'의 형태로 쓰인다. 최상급의 비교 표현은 '최상급 + of[in]…'의 형태를 사용한다.

최상급

① **형용사 / 부사의 원급 + -est**

deepest   shortest   wisest

② **most + 원급**

most important   most interesting   most useful

최상급의 비교 표현

This lake is <u>the deep</u>est <u>in</u> the world.　　원급 + -est

Repetition is <u>the simple</u>st <u>of</u> all the tasks.　　e로 끝나는 단어 + -st

Summer is <u>the hott</u>est season <u>in</u> Korea.　　'단모음+단자음'으로 끝나는 단어+마지막 자음 한 개 더 쓰고 -est

This is the <u>easi</u>est recipe <u>in</u> the world.　　'자음+y'로 끝나는 단어+y를 i로 고치고 -est

Her lecture is <u>the</u> most <u>useful</u> in my school.　　'most+-ful, -less, -ous, -ive, -ing으로 끝나는 2음절 단어'

This one is <u>the</u> most important of all the formulas.　　'most+3음절 이상의 단어'

Activity 1

아래 표의 빈칸에 적절한 형태의 비교급 또는 최상급을 쓰세요.

형용사 / 부사	비교급	최상급
good		best
bad	worse	
hot	hotter	
large		
difficult		most difficult

Activity 2

다음 그림을 보고 빈칸에 알맞은 표현을 쓰세요.

비교급, 최상급 표현은 괄호 안의 표현을 활용하세요.

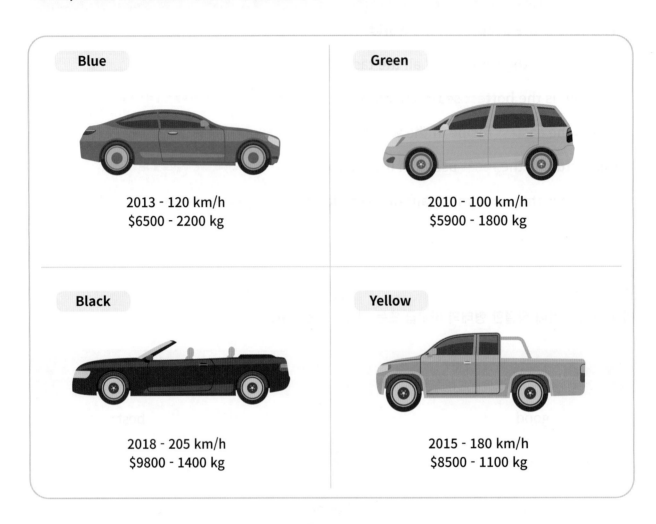

Blue
2013 - 120 km/h
$6500 - 2200 kg

Green
2010 - 100 km/h
$5900 - 1800 kg

Black
2018 - 205 km/h
$9800 - 1400 kg

Yellow
2015 - 180 km/h
$8500 - 1100 kg

❶ The blue car is _____ (expensive) than the green car.

❷ The _____ car is cheaper than the blue car.

❸ The blue car is the _____ (heavy) car.

❹ The yellow car is _____ (old) than the black car.

❺ The _____ car is the lightest car.

❻ The _____ car is the fastest and _____ (expensive) car.

Exercise 1

알맞은 단어를 골라 문장을 완성하세요.

❶ He is   **tall / taller**   than me.

❷ A rabbit is   **faster / fastest**   than a turtle.

❸ The house is the   **bigger / biggest**   building in our city.

❹ Understanding is more   **important / importanter**   than memorizing.

❺ She is the   **more / most**   attractive woman in the party.

Exercise 2

보기의 단어를 적절한 형태로 활용하여, 빈칸에 알맞은 단어를 쓰세요.

보기   wise   most   more   interesting   high

❶ It is the most _____ part of this book.
그것은 이 책에서 가장 흥미로운 부분이다.

❷ The mountain is _____ than the tower.
그 산은 그 타워보다 더 높다.

❸ Sometimes, young people are _____ than seniors.
때때로, 젊은 사람들이 나이가 많은 사람들보다 현명하다.

❹ They are in the _____ difficult time in their life.
그들은 인생에서 가장 힘든 시기에 있다.

❺ It is _____ useful information than what we had.
그것은 우리가 가지고 있던 정보보다 더욱 유용하다.

✏️ Sentence Completion ━━━━━━━━━━━━━━━━

1 A: The bear is the ⬚⬚⬚⬚⬚ animal
   in the zoo.
   B: I want to see it.

(A) big
(B) bigger
(C) biggest
(D) most biggest

4 A: We can see birds easily.
   B: Birds are the most ⬚⬚⬚⬚⬚
      animal in the community.

(A) common
(B) commonly
(C) commoner
(D) commonest

2 A: He is ⬚⬚⬚⬚⬚ than other
   students.
   B: He is the strongest man in our school.

(A) strong
(B) stronger
(C) strongest
(D) more stronger

5 A: Which item is the ⬚⬚⬚⬚⬚
      valuable in the store?
   B: Maybe, our diamond is.

(A) too
(B) very
(C) most
(D) more

3 A: I can't understand it.
   B: We can think more ⬚⬚⬚⬚⬚ .

(A) clear
(B) clearly
(C) clearer
(D) clearest

6 A: It is   interesting than
    the book.

   B: I think so too.

(A) a

(B) an

(C) most

(D) more

9 A: The dot is the most
    feature of the clothes.

   B: That's great.

(A) strike

(B) striked

(C) striken

(D) striking

7 A: She is the   students in
    our class

   B: She knows everything.

(A) smart

(B) smarter

(C) smartest

(D) smarting

10 A: How much is it?

   B: It is the   expensive one
    in our shop.

(A) so

(B) very

(C) more

(D) most

8 A: I couldn't sleep last night.

   B: Sleeping is   important
    than we may think.

(A) so

(B) very

(C) more

(D) most

✏️ Writing Activity

1 **more**
더 많은 수[양]

more

2 **most**
최대의

most

3 **interest**
관심, 흥미

interest

4 **large**
큰

large

5 **worse**
더 나쁜

worse

6 important
중요한

important

7 attractive
매력적인

attractive

8 cheap
싼

cheap

9 useful
유용한

useful

10 difficult
어려운

difficult

Unit Review

배운 내용 스스로 정리해보기

❶ 비교급

비교급은 두 가지를 비교하는 데 사용되며 ❶ [   ] 또는 ❷ [   ] 의 형태로 쓰인다. 비교급의 비교 표현은 '비교급+than…'의 형태를 사용한다.

예시문장 써보기

① 형용사/부사의 원급+er

➜ _____

② more+원급

➜ _____

❷ 최상급

최상급은 세 가지 이상을 비교하는 데 쓰이며 ❶ [   ] 또는 ❷ [   ] 의 형태로 쓰인다. 최상급의 비교 표현은 '최상급+of[in]…'의 형태를 사용한다.

예시문장 써보기

① 형용사/부사의 원급+-est

➜ _____

② most+원급

➜ _____

TOSEL 실전문제 ④

SECTION II. Reading and Writing

PART A. Sentence Completion

DIRECTIONS: For questions 1 to 20, fill in the blanks to complete the sentences. Choose the option that BEST completes each blank.

지시 사항: 1번부터 20번까지는 빈칸을 알맞게 채워 대화를 완성하는 문제입니다. 가장 알맞은 답을 고르세요.

1. A: He always gets up _____.
   B: He is a diligent person.

   (A) earl
   (B) late
   (C) early
   (D) lately

2. A: He is the _____ student in his class.
   B: His height is almost 180cm.

   (A) tall
   (B) taller
   (C) talled
   (D) tallest

3. A: I want to have _____ money.
   B: What are you going to do with the money?

   (A) few
   (B) little
   (C) much
   (D) many

4. A: Where is she?
   B: She _____ goes to the library after school.

   (A) rarely
   (B) never
   (C) seldom
   (D) usually

5. A: Summer is _____ than spring.
   B: I don't like hot weather.

   (A) hot
   (B) hots
   (C) hotter
   (D) hottest

6. A: Where is he going?
   B: He _____ to the swimming pool before dinner.

   (A) is always

   (B) always go

   (C) go always

   (D) always goes

7. A: She is studying hard.
   B: She bought _____ books at the bookstore.

   (A) a

   (B) an

   (C) much

   (D) many

8. A: _____, I can ride the rollercoaster.
   B: That's great.

   (A) Very

   (B) Even

   (C) Loudly

   (D) Fortunately

9. A: I found only _____ errors.
   B: Then, print it now.

   (A) few

   (B) little

   (C) much

   (D) many

10. A: He is the _____ important player in our school.
    B: I agree.

    (A) more

    (B) most

    (C) many

    (D) much

11. A: She made it look _____.
    B: I don't know how she did it.

    (A) easy

    (B) easily

    (C) easier

    (D) easiest

14. A: He is more _____ than others in
        there.
    B: His songs are so popular.

    (A) famous

    (B) famouser

    (C) famousest

    (D) the famous

12. A: He _____ studies hard.
    B: But, the exam is coming.

    (A) often

    (B) rarely

    (C) always

    (D) usually

15. A: She _____ loves him.
    B: I hope they will go well.

    (A) true

    (B) hard

    (C) truely

    (D) hardly

13. A: We don't have much _____.
    B: Ok, I'll do it right away.

    (A) time

    (B) times

    (C) timed

    (D) timing

16. A: Cheetahs can run _____.
    B: They are the fastest animal!

    (A) fast

    (B) fastly

    (C) faster

    (D) fastest

19. A: I think it is a little pricey.
    B: How about this? It's _____.

    (A) cheap

    (B) cheaper

    (C) more cheap

    (D) more cheaper

17. A: I lost _____ money.
    B: Oh, what happened?

    (A) lots

    (B) a lot

    (C) much

    (D) many

20. A: He _____ angry.
    B: I know. He is so patient.

    (A) never get

    (B) get never

    (C) gets never

    (D) never gets

18. A: Was the mall crowded?
    B: Yes, there were _____ people.

    (A) one

    (B) a lot

    (C) lots of

    (D) a many of

CHAPTER 05

V. 접속사와 전치사

UNIT 01

단어를 연결하는 접속사

and	비슷한 의미의 단어 두 개를 연결할 때
but	반대되는 의미의 단어 두 개를 연결할 때
or	두 단어 중 하나를 선택할 때

experiment	실험	popular	인기 있는
easy	쉬운	proud	자랑스러워하는
huge	큰, 거대한	set	놓다
tasty	맛있는	product	상품
forecast	예측, 예보	rise	증가

등위 접속사 and, but, or는 **문법적 기능이 같은 단어**를 연결한다.

❶ and

'...고', '...와'라는 의미로 **서로 비슷한 단어**를 연결할 때 쓰인다.

> He ate <u>an apple</u> and <u>a banana</u> today.
> 　　　　명사　　　　　　　명사
>
> <u>He</u> and <u>I</u> are proud of you.
> 대명사　　　대명사
>
> The first experiment was <u>easy</u> and <u>exciting</u>.
> 　　　　　　　　　　　　형용사　　　　형용사
>
> The weather forecast predicts <u>cold</u> and <u>rainy</u> weather.
> 　　　　　　　　　　　　　　형용사　　　　형용사
>
> The <u>huge</u> and <u>bright</u> sun rises every day.
> 　　　형용사　　　　형용사

❷ but

'...지만', '...(으)나'라는 의미로 **서로 대조되는 단어**를 연결할 때 쓰인다.

> This movie is <u>popular</u> but <u>boring</u>.
> 　　　　　　　형용사　　　　형용사
>
> The food is <u>tasty</u> but <u>expensive</u>.
> 　　　　　　형용사　　　　형용사
>
> She was <u>very young</u> but <u>very wise</u>.
> 　　　　　　형용사　　　　형용사
>
> The police officer chased the man <u>silently</u> but <u>fast</u>.
> 　　　　　　　　　　　　　　　　부사　　　　부사
>
> Wayne <u>bought</u> but <u>refunded</u> the product.
> 　　　동사　　　　　동사

❸ <u>or</u>

'또는[혹은]'이라는 의미로 둘 중 하나를 선택할 때 쓰인다.

> Is the story <u>true</u> or <u>false</u>?
> 형용사   형용사
>
> Is your younger sister <u>taller</u> or <u>smaller</u> than you?
>   형용사   형용사
>
> Is your nickname "<u>a cat</u>" or "<u>a dog</u>"?
>   명사   명사
>
> <u>He</u> or <u>she</u> will visit your house tomorrow.
> 대명사 대명사
>
> He asked her whether to set the table <u>here</u> or <u>there</u>.
>   부사   부사

Activity 1

다음 접속사의 적절한 우리말 뜻에 연결해보세요.

and	●	●	...지만, …(으)나
or	●	●	또는, 혹은
but	●	●	…고, …와

Activity 2

미로판에서 다음 단어로부터 알맞은 접속사를 가지고 적절한 단어 모음을 완성하세요.

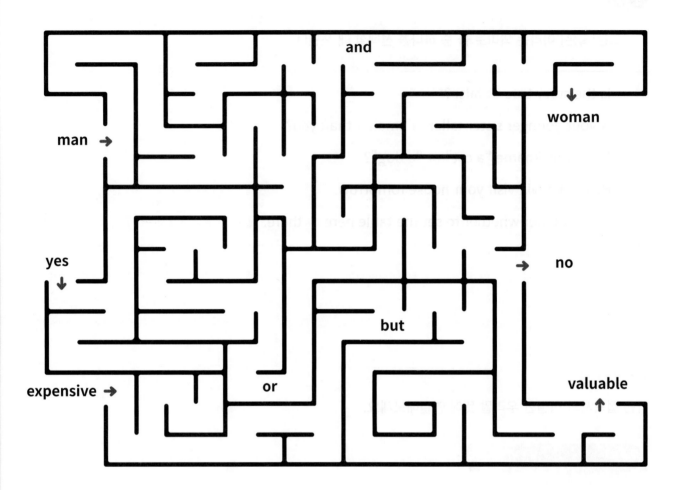

Exercise 1

알맞은 단어를 골라 문장을 완성하세요.

❶ He is handsome   **and / but**   tall.

❷ The room is clean   **or / but**   small.

❸ She is smart   **but / and**   selfish.

❹ Jane   **and / or**   Kane are siblings.

❺ Which one do you like? Beef   **but / or**   pork?

Exercise 2

다음 우리말에 맞게 빈칸에 알맞은 단어를 쓰세요.

❶ Tiger _____ lion is the king of the animals.
호랑이 또는 사자가 동물의 왕이다.

❷ We climbed the mountain _____ shouted at the top.
우리는 산에 올랐고 정상에서 소리쳤다.

❸ He is good at soccer _____ is not good at studying.
그는 축구를 잘하지만 공부를 잘하지는 못한다.

❹ Our teacher called me _____ Jenny.
우리 선생님은 나와 Jenny를 불렀다.

❺ You have to go to the hospital _____ take a rest.
너는 병원에 가거나 쉬어야만 한다.

Sentence Completion

1 A: The festival is popular _____ famous.

   B: Have you been there?

   (A) or
   (B) so
   (C) but
   (D) and

2 A: When is he coming back?

   B: He may come on Friday _____ Saturday.

   (A) or
   (B) so
   (C) but
   (D) and

3 A: There is a tree in the middle.

   B: The tree is huge _____ old.

   (A) or
   (B) so
   (C) to
   (D) but

4 A: I'm thirsty.

   B: We can order a glass of juice _____ coffee.

   (A) or
   (B) so
   (C) but
   (D) and

5 A: He will write and _____ an email to you.

   B: Ok, Thanks.

   (A) sent
   (B) send
   (C) sends
   (D) sending

6 A: She ran and _____ to the finish line.

B: Did she win first place?

(A) jump
(B) jumps
(C) jumped
(D) jumping

9 A: What did you eat for lunch?

B: We ate both hamburger _____ french fries.

(A) or
(B) so
(C) but
(D) and

7 A: You can choose the play mode: easy or _____.

B: I'll choose the easy one.

(A) hard
(B) easily
(C) hardly
(D) simple

10 A: Do you prefer checks _____ dots?

B: I prefer checked clothes.

(A) or
(B) so
(C) but
(D) and

8 A: There _____ man and woman on the deck of cruise.

B: The fireworks will start soon.

(A) is
(B) are
(C) was
(D) were

1 **experiment**
실험

experiment

2 **easy**
쉬운

easy

3 **huge**
큰, 거대한

huge

4 **tasty**
맛있는

tasty

5 **forecast**
예측, 예보

forecast

6 popular
인기 있는

popular

7 proud
자랑스러워하는

proud

8 set
놓다

set

9 product
상품

product

10 rise
증가

rise

Unit Review

배운 내용 스스로 정리해보기

❶ <u>and</u>

and는 '...고', '...와'라는 의미로 서로 _____ 단어를 연결할 때 쓰인다.

예시문장 써보기

① 명사와 명사 연결

➔ _____

② 형용사와 형용사 연결

➔ _____

❷ <u>but</u>

but은 '...지만', '...(으)나'라는 의미로 서로 ❶ _____ 단어를 연결할 때 쓰인다.

예시문장 써보기

① 형용사와 형용사 연결

➔ _____

② 부사와 부사 연결

➔ _____

❸ <u>or</u>

or는 '또는[혹은]'이라는 의미로 둘 중 하나를 ❶ _____ 할 때 쓰인다.

예시문장 써보기

① 명사와 명사 연결

➔ _____

② 형용사와 형용사 연결

➔ _____

UNIT 02

——

문장을 연결하는 접속사

등위접속사	앞뒤 문장이 서로 대등한 관계일 때
종속접속사	앞뒤 문장이 서로 대등하지 않은 관계일 때

tent	텐트	hug	안다
crawl	기다	wallet	지갑
creative	창의적인	serve	제공하다
foggy	안개가 낀	follow	따라가다
hamper	방해하다	cure	낫게 하다

❶ 등위접속사

등위접속사는 **문법적 기능이 같은 절을** 연결한다.

and: '...와', '그리고', '그래서'

We pitched a tent and (we) had a barbecue.

My twins crawled and (they) hugged each other.

but: '하지만', '그러나'

Someone stole my wallet but I found it soon.

Tom served us dinner but all of the food was spicy.

or: '또는', '그렇지 않으면'

Jane went to Rosie's house or (she) stayed at her home.

Start now, or you lose your opportunities.

so: '그래서', '그러므로'

I won the first prize, so I was very happy.

The general was very brave, so I followed him.

❷ 종속접속사

종속접속사는 종속절을 주절에 연결한다

when: '...(할) 때'

When I arrived at the hospital, the doctor was curing her patient.

I first met David when I was ten years old.

before: '...(하기) 전에'

You should brush your teeth before you go to bed.

Before the exam finished, I solved all of the questions.

after: '...(한) 후에'

My cousin hampered me after he finished his homework.

After I took a shower, I wore my school uniform.

because: '...때문에'

Because it was foggy yesterday, the school bus arrived late.

Because Ella is creative, she always makes a great invention.

Activity 1

다음 접속사의 적절한 우리말 뜻에 연결해보세요.

before	●	●	…(할) 때
after	●	●	… 때문에
so	●	●	…(하기) 전에
when	●	●	그래서, 그러므로
because	●	●	…(한) 이후에

Activity 2

다음 퍼즐에서 접속사를 찾으세요. (5개)

```
A   N   H   T   A   L   W   B
O   L   P   O   B   T   E   E
S   U   W   H   E   N   Q   C
B   N   H   A   F   T   L   A
B   U   V   E   O   O   C   U
A   F   T   E   R   S   M   S
S   E   L   D   E   M   S   E
C   R   C   O   F   T   Y   S
```

Exercise 1

알맞은 단어를 골라 문장을 완성하세요.

❶   **After / Before**   you finish your homework, you can watch TV.

❷ He was a shy boy   **because / when**   he was young.

❸ Show your ticket   **and / or**   you can not enter there

❹ She passed the exam   **but / so**   I was happy.

❺   **Because / Before**   the exam is tomorrow, we will go to the library.

Exercise 2

다음 우리말에 맞게 빈칸에 알맞은 단어를 쓰세요.

❶ She studies hard _____ she wants to be a doctor.
그녀는 의사가 되고 싶기 때문에 공부를 열심히 한다.

❷ It is a new model _____ it has a lot of errors.
이것은 새로운 모델이지만 많은 오류를 가지고 있다.

❸ You should speak loud _____ other people can't hear you.
너는 크게 말해야 한다, 그렇지 않으면 다른 사람들이 듣지 못한다.

❹ _____ I saw the newspaper, I didn't know what had happened.
신문을 보기 전에, 나는 무슨 일이 일어났는지 알지 못했다.

❺ _____ he finished his studies, he went to America.
그는 공부를 마친 후, 미국으로 갔다.

1. A: How is she doing?

   B: She graduated from university

   _____ had no job.

   (A) or

   (B) so

   (C) but

   (D) and

4. A: Did you see the movie?

   B: Yes, but I won't spoil the ending

   _____ you see it.

   (A) after

   (B) when

   (C) before

   (D) because

2. A: Who is the man?

   B: He is our teacher _____ he is my uncle.

   (A) and

   (B) after

   (C) when

   (D) before

5. A: The singer is coming.

   B: He will sing a song _____ play guitar.

   (A) so

   (B) or

   (C) and

   (D) when

3. A: How can he submit his assignment?

   B: _____ he was my friend, I helped him.

   (A) So

   (B) After

   (C) When

   (D) Because

6 A: She became a famous dancer.

B: _____ she was young, she was talented in dancing.

(A) So

(B) But

(C) When

(D) Because

9 A: What do I do next?

B: _____ you make it, add some soy sauce.

(A) after

(B) when

(C) before

(D) because

7 A: It's so hot in the house.

B: _____ we fix the air conditioner, we can turn it on.

(A) And

(B) After

(C) Before

(D) Because

10 A: He jumped over the obstacle and _____ to the finish line.

B: He was so fast.

(A) run

(B) ran

(C) runner

(D) running

8 A: I reviewed the book, _____ couldn't find any mistakes.

B: Ok, we should print it by tomorrow.

(A) but

(B) and

(C) after

(D) when

1 **tent**
텐트

2 **crawl**
기다

3 **creative**
창의적인

4 **foggy**
안개가 낀

5 **hamper**
방해하다

6   **hug**
안다

hug

7   **wallet**
지갑

wallet

8   **serve**
제공하다

serve

9   **follow**
따라가다

follow

10   **cure**
낫게 하다

cure

Unit Review

배운 내용 스스로 정리해보기

❶ 등위접속사

등위접속사는 ❶ [   ] 절을 연결한다.

예시문장 써보기

① and ➜ _____

② but ➜ _____

③ so ➜ _____

❷ 종속접속사

종속접속사는 ❶ [   ] (을)를 ❷ [   ] 에 연결한다.

예시문장 써보기

① when ➜ _____

② before ➜ _____

③ because ➜ _____

UNIT 03

—

시간과 장소를 나타내는 전치사

시간	in, at, on	before, after 등 시간표현과 쓰임
장소		above, below 등 장소표현과 쓰임

vacation	방학	station	정류장
noon	정오	office	사무실
night	밤	airport	공항
past	과거	beach	해변
tomorrow	내일	road	도로

UNIT **3** 시간과 장소를 나타내는 전치사

❶ 시간

in	연도, 월, 계절, 오전, 오후, 아침, 점심, 저녁 등 He was born in 2009.
at	시각, 시점, 하루 중 일부 등 They met at night/ eight o'clock.
on	요일, 특정한 날 등 I saw him on Tuesday.
before	'...전에' My cell phone should ring before noon.
after	'...후에' It will be cold after tomorrow.
for	'...동안 (시간의 길이)' He built the weather museum for the past two years.
during	'...동안 (특정 기간)' Sara will stay on the beach during the vacation.
till (until)	'...까지 (계속)' The crowd waited for Grace at the station till[until] seven.
by	'...까지 (완료)' You should submit the homework by next Wednesday.

❷ 장소

in	비교적 넓은 공간의 내부 She studied English in London.

at	비교적 좁은 공간이나 지점, 번지 I will stay at my office.
on	접촉면 위 I put the key on the table.
above	'위쪽에' The airplane was flying above the clouds.
below	'아래쪽에' The score was below the average.
over	'(일직선상으로 바로) 위에' There is a rainbow over the mountain.
under	'(일직선상으로 바로) 아래에' Newton found the law of gravity under an apple tree.

Activity 1

다음 전치사의 적절한 우리말 뜻에 연결해보세요.

for	●	●	아래에
above	●	●	… 까지 (계속)
till	●	●	…동안(시간의 길이)
below	●	●	…동안(특정 기간)
during	●	●	위쪽에

Activity 2

다음 보기를 활용하여 전치사와 알맞은 말을 사다리 밑에 쓰세요.

보기   9 o'clock   the morning   summer vacation
Wednesday   one hour

on	in	at	during	for

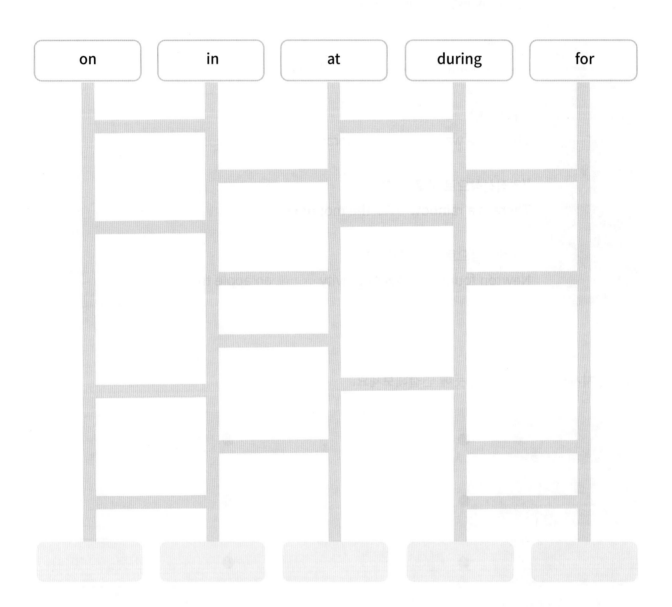

Exercise 1

알맞은 단어를 골라 문장을 완성하세요.

❶ We went to China **during / above** the vacation.

❷ She is waiting **below / at** the bus station.

❸ You should come back home **above / before** nightfall.

❹ His weight is **above / for** the average.

❺ Return the book **on / by** tomorrow.

Exercise 2

다음 보기를 활용하여, 우리말에 맞게 빈칸에 알맞은 단어를 쓰세요.

보기   under   above   on   by   for

❶ There are many cars   the road.
도로 위에 많은 차들이 있다.

❷ We will go to the airport   9 a.m.
우리는 오전 9시까지 공항에 갈 것이다.

❸ The water comes   our chests.
물이 우리의 가슴 위까지 올라온다.

❹   about 2 years, men must do military duty.
대략 2년 동안, 남자들은 군복무를 해야만 한다.

❺ He dropped his smartphone   the bed.
그는 그의 휴대폰을 침대 아래에 떨어뜨렸다.

Sentence Completion

1 A: _____ the summer season, there are many people in the hotel.

B: It is hard to reserve.

(A) In
(B) On
(C) For
(D) During

2 A: Where can I put these books?

B: Put it _____ the shelf.

(A) in
(B) at
(C) on
(D) under

3 A: It will be raining _____ dinner.

B: It is good to go back home before night.

(A) in
(B) after
(C) above
(D) before

4 A: They climbed _____ the fence.

B: That's not good.

(A) at
(B) over
(C) below
(D) under

5 A: Bake _____ the crust is crispy.

B: Ok, I got it.

(A) at
(B) until
(C) after
(D) during

6 A: Where is the department store?

B: It is _____ nearby post office.

(A) at

(B) on

(C) over

(D) under

9 A: Who is he?

B: I don't know. He hides his face _____ the mask.

(A) for

(B) over

(C) under

(D) below

7 A: We will meet _____ noon.

B: Can I join you?

(A) in

(B) on

(C) above

(D) before

10 A: The souvenir shop will be open _____ 5 P.M.

B: We have to hurry.

(A) at

(B) over

(C) after

(D) until

8 A: Where is my textbook?

B: _____ the bookshelf, you can find it.

(A) At

(B) Above

(C) Before

(D) During

1 **vacation**
방학

2 **noon**
정오

3 **night**
밤

4 **past**
과거

5 **tomorrow**
내일

6 station
정류장

7 office
사무실

8 airport
공항

9 beach
해변

10 road
도로

Unit Review

배운 내용 스스로 정리해보기

❶ 시간

예시문장 써보기

① in ➜ _____

② at ➜ _____

③ on ➜ _____

④ for ➜ _____

❷ 장소

예시문장 써보기

① in ➜ _____

② at ➜ _____

③ on ➜ _____

④ over ➜ _____

UNIT 04

—

그 밖의 전치사

with	'...(으)로', '...을(를) 가지고', '...와 함께'
by	'...에 의하여', '...(으)로'
on	'...에 대한'

desert	사막	museum	박물관
town	(소)도시	foreign	외국의
building	건물	cellphone	휴대전화
church	교회	increase	증가하다
crowd	사람들, 군중	weather	날씨

with	'...(으)로', '...을(를) 가지고', '...와 함께'
	The town is covered with snow.
	He cut the fish with a knife.
	I went to the weather museum with my friends.
without	'...없이'
	Teachers wouldn't exist without students.
	I can do it without your help.
by	'...에 의하여', '...(으)로'
	The crowd was upset by the mayor.
	I go to church by car.
from	'...(으)로 만들어지다(화학적 변화)', '...부터'
	Paper is made from wood.
	Pottery is made from soil.
of	'...의', '...에 대한', '...(으)로 만들어지다(물리적 변화)', '~로부터'
	She is a friend of mine.
	I always think of you.
	The chair is made of wood.
	This building is made of bricks.
due to	'...때문에', '...(으)로 인하여'
	This cell phone is popular due to its speed.
	Our productivity increased due to the change.

about	'...에 대한'
	I read a book about the desert.
	Do you know about the news?
on	'...에 대한', '...으로', '...에 의하여'
	He borrowed a book on foreign cultures.
	We debated on the subject.

Activity 1

다음 전치사의 적절한 우리말 뜻에 연결해보세요.

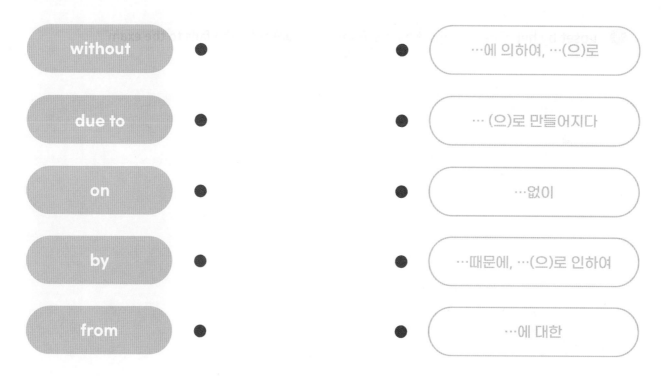

without	…에 의하여, …(으)로
due to	… (으)로 만들어지다
on	…없이
by	…때문에, …(으)로 인하여
from	…에 대한

Activity 2

다음 중 부적절한 전치사가 들어간 경우를 고르세요.

❶ by car   by bus   by go

❷ Due to its speed   Due to it is heavy   Due to its thickness

❸ made about soil   made of soil   made from soil

❹ book on history   book at history   book about history

❺ upset by her sister   upset by her friend   upset by she fails to the exam

Exercise 1

알맞은 단어를 골라 문장을 완성하세요.

❶ We can't go on a picnic   due to / on   the bad weather.

❷ He went to the town   by / with   train.

❸ They are talking   of / about   foreign culture.

❹ The factory runs   due to / on   solar energy.

❺ The shoes are one   of / by   my treasures.

Exercise 2

다음 보기를 활용하여, 우리말에 맞게 빈칸에 알맞은 단어를 쓰세요.

| 보기 | without | due to | from | by | of |

❶ He can be a lawyer _____ passing the test.
그는 시험에 통과함으로써 변호사가 될 수 있다.

❷ I can't live _____ you.
너 없이는 살 수가 없다.

❸ _____ global warming, the weather is getting hot.
지구 온난화 때문에, 날씨가 점점 더워진다.

❹ Most petroleum is imported _____ other countries.
대부분의 석유는 다른 나라로부터 수입된다.

❺ She thinks _____ me as a smart student.
그녀는 나를 똑똑한 학생으로 생각한다.

Sentence Completion

1 A: Why don't you go to the museum
   _____ my friends?
   B: Oh, that's great.

(A) of
(B) with
(C) about
(D) without

2 A: What are you reading?
   B: I'm reading a book _____
      Korean history.

(A) on
(B) by
(C) from
(D) due to

3 A: He is one _____ my brothers.
   B: How many brothers do you have?

(A) of
(B) on
(C) with
(D) about

4 A: I can go to work _____ foot.
   B: I envy you.

(A) on
(B) by
(C) from
(D) without

5 A: She studied hard _____
      a break.
   B: She should be tired.

(A) of
(B) by
(C) from
(D) without

6 A: What is the subject of discussion?

B: We will talk _____ gender discrimination.

(A) of

(B) by

(C) with

(D) about

7 A: Why are you late?

B: I'm late _____ the traffic jam.

(A) on

(B) with

(C) from

(D) due to

8 A: Cactus can live a long time _____ water.

B: It's different from other plants.

(A) with

(B) about

(C) due to

(D) without

9 A: Today, we'll learn _____ American culture.

B: It seems quite interesting.

(A) at

(B) by

(C) from

(D) about

10 A: Where is the exit _____ this building?

B: You can see another gate next to the souvenir shop.

(A) of

(B) by

(C) with

(D) from

1 **desert**
사막

desert

2 **town**
(소)도시

town

3 **building**
건물

building

4 **church**
교회

church

5 **crowd**
사람들, 군중

crowd

6 **museum**
박물관

7 **foreign**
외국의

8 **cellphone**
휴대전화

9 **increase**
증가하다

10 **weather**
날씨

그 밖의 전치사

예시문장 써보기

① with ➔ _____

② without ➔ _____

③ by ➔ _____

④ from ➔ _____

⑤ of ➔ _____

⑥ due to ➔ _____

⑦ about ➔ _____

TOSEL 실전문제 ⑤

SECTION II. Reading and Writing

PART A. Sentence Completion

DIRECTIONS: For questions 1 to 20, fill in the blanks to complete the sentences. Choose the option that BEST completes each blank.

지시 사항: 1번부터 20번까지는 빈칸을 알맞게 채워 대화를 완성하는 문제입니다. 가장 알맞은 답을 고르세요.

1. A: He is handsome _____ selfish.
   B: I don't like him.

   (A) or

   (B) so

   (C) but

   (D) and

2. A: _____ she was young, she was good at drawing.
   B: She is so versatile.

   (A) After

   (B) What

   (C) When

   (D) Because

3. A: You can't go in _____ your parents.
   B: Ok, I'll be back next time.

   (A) with

   (B) from

   (C) due to

   (D) without

4. A: We will meet _____ dinner.
   B: Ok, I'll go about 8 p.m.

   (A) on

   (B) after

   (C) before

   (D) during

5. A: Study hard now _____ you can't be a doctor.
   B: But, it's too boring.

   (A) or

   (B) so

   (C) but

   (D) and

6. A: What will you do _____ summer vacation?
   B: My family will go abroad to Europe.

   (A) at

   (B) by

   (C) until

   (D) during

9. A: When is the deadline?
   B: You should submit the assignment _____ next Monday.

   (A) in

   (B) on

   (C) by

   (D) after

7. A: Your puppy is small _____ cute.
   B: He is my treasure.

   (A) or

   (B) so

   (C) but

   (D) and

10. A: Do you want some juice _____ milk?
    B: I want to drink apple juice.

    (A) or

    (B) of

    (C) but

    (D) and

8. A: How can we get there?
   B: We may go _____ train.

   (A) of

   (B) by

   (C) from

   (D) about

11. A: We can't go to the park _____ the bad weather.
    B: Yes, We should go another day.

    (A) by

    (B) with

    (C) about

    (D) due to

12. A: Wash your hands _____ you come in.
    B: Ok, I'll do that.

    (A) or

    (B) and

    (C) after

    (D) because

13. A: The movie runs _____ three hours.
    B: It's too long.

    (A) on

    (B) for

    (C) before

    (D) during

14. A: He is a quiet _____ active student.
    B: He gets along well with his friends.

    (A) or

    (B) and

    (C) but

    (D) because

15. A: I borrowed a book _____ Korean history.
    B: It's quite interesting.

    (A) on

    (B) by

    (C) under

    (D) from

16. A: What did you do?
    B: We went ice fishing _____ skiing.

    (A) if

    (B) so

    (C) but

    (D) and

17. A: _____ of heavy traffic, it took longer.
    B: That's okay.

    (A) Or

    (B) But

    (C) And

    (D) Because

18. A: When does the new semester start?
    B: _____ September 2nd.

    (A) In

    (B) At

    (C) On

    (D) Behind

19. A: Please come _____ 4:30.
    B: Can I be there by 4:45?

    (A) in

    (B) at

    (C) on

    (D) from

20. A: How was the party yesterday?
    B: It wasn't fun _____ you.

    (A) of

    (B) by

    (C) from

    (D) without

CHAPTER 06

VI. 문장

UNIT 01

문장의 형식

1형식	주어 + 동사
2형식	주어 + 동사 + 보어
3형식	주어 + 동사 + 목적어

mail	우편	contain	~이 들어있다
gallery	미술관	free	자유로운
review	검토	improve	개선되다
sale	판매	native	태어난 곳의
company	회사	own	자신의

UNIT **1** 문장의 형식

❶ 1형식

주어 + 완전자동사 (S + V)

Time flies.
<u>S</u> <u>V</u>

The sun rises in the east.
<u>S</u> <u>V</u>

A lot of birds sing on the trees.
<u>S</u> <u>V</u>

Thomas came early.
<u>S</u> <u>V</u>

Peter lives in the town.
<u>S</u> <u>V</u>

Car sales fell in August.
<u>S</u> <u>V</u>

❷ 2형식

주어 + 불완전자동사 + 주격보어 (S + V + S.C.)

She is a native speaker.
<u>S</u> <u>V</u> <u>C</u>

I am free for dinner.
<u>S</u> <u>V</u> <u>C</u>

The children kept quiet.
<u>S</u> <u>V</u> <u>C</u>

The gallery became a popular place.
<u>S</u> <u>V</u> <u>C</u>

He grows stronger every day.
<u>S</u> <u>V</u> <u>C</u>

His face turned pale.
<u>S</u> <u>V</u> <u>C</u>

❸ 3형식

The company improved their own environment.
S   V   O

I opened the mail yesterday.
S   V   O

He prepared lunch.
S   V   O

The box contains a gift.
S   V   O

The teacher reviewed a lot of reports during the weekend.
S   V   O

I bought a new jacket.
S   V   O

Activity 1

다음 형식에 적절한 문장을 연결해보세요.

1형식	●	●	I like you.
2형식	●	●	He is my teacher.
3형식	●	●	They came late.

Activity 2

1, 2, 3형식 모든 문장에 주어진 단어가 들어가도록 문장을 만들어 보세요.

girl

❶ 1형식 ➜ _____

❷ 2형식 ➜ _____

❸ 3형식 ➜ _____

puppy

❶ 1형식 ➜ _____

❷ 2형식 ➜ _____

❸ 3형식 ➜ _____

people

❶ 1형식 ➜ _____

❷ 2형식 ➜ _____

❸ 3형식 ➜ _____

Exercise 1

빈칸에 다음 문장이 어떤 형식인지 쓰세요.

❶ He sent an email to you. (   )

❷ She became a famous singer. (   )

❸ A lot of bears live in the forest. (   )

❹ The man is a creative scientist. (   )

❺ I love grilled bacon. (   )

Exercise 2

다음 문장에서 동사는 O표, 보어는 △표, 목적어는 □표 하세요.

❶ She teaches difficult science topics.
그녀는 어려운 과학 주제를 가르친다.

❷ He fell asleep on the sofa.
그는 소파 위에서 잠들었다.

❸ This seat is empty.
이 자리는 비어있다.

❹ They arrived at the hotel.
그들은 호텔에 도착했다.

❺ The palace was beautiful.
그 궁전은 아름다웠다.

Sentence Completion

1 A: How was the movie last night?

   B: It was so sad. I _____ after.

(A) cry
(B) cried
(C) crying
(D) am crying

4 A: Students are greeting _____ in the classroom.

   B: I don't know anyone here.

(A) he
(B) they
(C) other
(D) each other

2 A: What do you think about my hair?

   B: I think I like _____ .

(A) it
(B) its
(C) your
(D) they

5 A: I want to talk with the manager.

   B: Sorry, but he is _____ vacation.

(A) of
(B) in
(C) on
(D) out

3 A: What's the weather like?

   B: There _____ no clouds or wind.

(A) is
(B) be
(C) am
(D) are

6 A: What did you buy for her present?

B: I bought a small ⬚⬚⬚⬚⬚⬚⬚ .

(A) to

(B) her

(C) figure

(D) in the store

9 A: How much is the entry fee?

B: Entry to the party is ⬚⬚⬚⬚⬚⬚⬚ .

(A) fee

(B) free

(C) much

(D) cheaper

7 A: He is going to transfer to another school.

B: Oh, I ⬚⬚⬚⬚⬚⬚⬚ sorry for that.

(A) do

(B) am

(C) with

(D) have

10 A: I think I ⬚⬚⬚⬚⬚⬚⬚ a fever.

B: You should go to the hospital.

(A) am

(B) has

(C) had

(D) have

8 A: It's white outside.

B: Last night, a lot of snow ⬚⬚⬚⬚⬚⬚⬚ .

(A) is

(B) fell

(C) fall

(D) white

UNIT 1 문장의 형식

1 **mail**

우편

2 **gallery**

미술관

3 **review**

검토

4 **sale**

판매

5 **company**

회사

6 contain

~이 들어있다

~~contain~~

7 free

자유로운

~~free~~

8 improve

개선되다

~~improve~~

9 native

태어난 곳의

~~native~~

10 own

자신의

~~own~~

Unit Review

배운 내용 스스로 정리해보기

❶ 1형식

문장의 1형식은 ❶   으로 구성된다.

예시문장 써보기

① 1형식 문장

➜ _____

❷ 2형식

문장의 2형식은 ❶   으로 구성된다.

예시문장 써보기

① 2형식 문장

➜ _____

❷ 3형식

문장의 3형식은 ❶   으로 구성된다.

예시문장 써보기

① 3형식 문장

➜ _____

UNIT 02

명령문

평서문	주어 + 동사	내용을 서술하는 문장
명령문	주어(You)를 생략하고 동사 원형으로 시작	명령·요구·충고·금지 등을 나타내는 문장

tell	알리다, 말하다	score	점수
medicine	약	wait	기다리다
worry	걱정하다	change	바꾸다
junk	쓸모없는 물건	protect	보호하다
shoot	쏘다	send	보내다

명령문은 **명령·요구·충고·금지** 등을 나타내는 문장으로 보통 **주어를 생략**하고 **동사원형**으로 시작한다.

❶ 직접명령문

긍정명령문: 주어 (You) 생략 후 동사원형으로 시작

You must tell me the truth.

➡ Tell me the truth.

You must be careful!

➡ Be careful!

You must change your medicine.

➡ Change your medicine.

부정명령문: Don't + 동사원형 / Never + 동사원형

You must not worry about the score.

➡ Don't worry about the score.

You must not eat junk food.

➡ Don't eat junk food.

You must not jump on the wet floor.

➡ Never jump on the wet floor.

❷ 간접명령문

1인칭이나 3인칭에게 명령·요구·충고·금지 등을 하는 명령문이다. 긍정명령문은 'Let + 목적어 + 동사원형…'으로 시작하고 부정명령문은 'Don't let + 목적어 + 동사원형…'으로 시작한다.

긍정명령문: Let + 목적어 + 동사원형...

Let <u>the actor shoot</u> an arrow.

Let <u>us protect</u> wild animals.

Let <u>me introduce</u> myself.

Let <u>her wait</u> for a moment.

부정명령문: Don't let + 목적어 + 동사원형...

Don't let <u>him send</u> a gift to me.

Don't let <u>them run</u> in the hallway.

Don't let <u>me buy</u> new shoes.

Don't let <u>her go</u> to bed late.

Activity 1

다음 제시된 문장을 적절한 명령문에 연결해보세요.

You must wash your hands.　●　　　●　Be careful.

You must not worry about that.　●　　　●　Close the window.

You must be careful.　●　　　●　Wash your hands.

You must close the window.　●　　　●　Don't worry about that.

Activity 2

다음 보기를 활용하여 빈칸을 채워보세요.

보기   worry   wash   turn off   give

❶ _____ your hands.

❷ Don't _____ about it.

❸ _____ me some sandwiches.

❹ _____ the light.

Exercise 1

알맞은 단어를 골라 문장을 완성하세요.

❶ Let me introduce **myself /yourself** .

❷ **Do / Don't** eat junk food.

❸ **Tell / Telling** me the story.

❹ Never **jump / jumps** at night.

❺ Don't **worried / worry** about her.

Exercise 2

보기의 단어를 활용하여, 우리말에 맞게 빈칸에 알맞은 단어를 쓰세요.

보기   catch   go   alone   let   give

❶ Don't leave him _____ .
그를 혼자 두지 마라.

❷ _____ me a basket.
나에게 바구니를 줘라.

❸ Let the children _____ out together.
아이들이 함께 밖으로 나갈 수 있게 하라.

❹ Don't _____ her eat too much.
그녀가 너무 많이 먹지 못하게 하라.

❺ _____ me if you can.
할 수 있다면 나를 잡아봐라.

Sentence Completion

1 A: It's raining a lot outside.

   B: _____ the window.

(A) Close

(B) Closed

(C) Closes

(D) Closing

2 A: Don't _____ loudly in the library.

   B: Ok, I'll be careful.

(A) speak

(B) speaks

(C) speaked

(D) speaking

3 A: Don't let her go out _____.

   B: I'll go with her.

(A) lone

(B) alone

(C) lonely

(D) loneliness

4 A: Let us _____ if you can't attend the meeting.

   B: I'll call you later.

(A) vote

(B) make

(C) know

(D) mean

5 A: _____ me the right answer.

   B: I'll check the answer sheet.

(A) Tell

(B) Shot

(C) Know

(D) Calculate

6 A: How can we play the card game.

   B: _____ the card first.

   (A) Shuffle

   (B) Shuffling

   (C) Shamble

   (D) Shambling

9 A: Please _____ the lettuce out of my hamburger.

   B: Ok, I checked it.

   (A) cut

   (B) eat

   (C) take

   (D) push

7 A: Let them _____ their own diaries.

   B: That's a good idea.

   (A) read

   (B) write

   (C) speak

   (D) listen

10 A: Don't _____ a picture in the museum.

   B: Ok, I'll just see it.

   (A) let

   (B) put

   (C) take

   (D) have

8 A: When do we meet?

   B: Let me _____ my calendar.

   (A) check

   (B) checks

   (C) checked

   (D) checking

UNIT 2 명령문

1 **tell**
알리다, 말하다

tell

2 **medicine**
약

medicine

3 **worry**
걱정하다

worry

4 **junk**
쓸모없는 물건

junk

5 **shoot**
쏘다

shoot

6 **score**
점수

7 **wait**
기다리다

8 **change**
바꾸다

9 **protect**
보호하다

10 **send**
보내다

Unit Review

배운 내용 스스로 정리해보기

❶ 직접명령문

직접명령문은 ❶ [   ]에게 직접 명령·요구·충고·금지 등을 하는 명령문이다.
긍정명령문은 보통 주어(You)를 생략하고 ❷ [   ](으)로 시작하고
부정명령문은 ❸ [   ] 또는 ❹ [   ](으)로 시작한다.

예시문장 써보기

① 긍정명령문 ➜ _____

② 부정명령문 ➜ _____

❷ 간접명령문

간접명령문은 ❶ [   ](이)나 ❷ [   ]에게 명령·요구·충고·금지 등을 하는
명령문이다. 긍정명령문은 ❸ [   ]으로 시작하고 부정명령문은
❹ [   ]으로 시작한다.

예시문장 써보기

① 긍정명령문

➜ _____

② 부정명령문

➜ _____

UNIT 03

의문문

평서문	주어 + 동사	내용을 서술하는 문장
의문문	동사 + 주어	❶ 의문사가 있는 의문문(Who, When, Where, What, Why, Which, How) ❷ 의문사가 없는 의문문 ❸ 조동사 의문문

graduate	졸업하다	restaurant	식당, 레스토랑
allow	허락하다	plan	계획
legend	전설	stranger	낯선 사람
dinner	저녁	allow	허락하다
answer	답	wish	원하다, 바라다

UNIT 3 의문문

❶ 의문사가 있는 의문문

'의문사(Who, When, Where, What, Why, Which, How 등)를 사용한 문장으로 Yes/No로 대답 할 수 없다.

be동사	'의문사+be동사+주어⋯?' '의문사(주어)+be동사⋯?' • A: What is your wish? B: My wish is to see my grandmother. • What is wrong?
일반 동사	'의문사+do[does/did]+주어+동사원형⋯?' '의문사(주어)+일반동사⋯?' • When did you eat dinner? • Who knows about this legend?
조동사	'의문사+조동사+주어+동사원형⋯?' '의문사(주어)+조동사+동사원형⋯?' • How can I go to the restaurant? • Who can answer this question?

❷ 의문사가 없는 의문문

의문사를 사용하지 않은 문장으로 Yes/No로 대답할 수 있다.

be동사	'be동사+주어⋯?'
	   A: Are you happy now?
	   B: Yes, I'm happy. / No, I'm not happy.
	 Isn't he handsome?

일반 동사	'Do[Does/Did]+주어+동사원형⋯?' Did you graduate from here? Don't you like this electric bicycle?

❸ 조동사 의문문

'조동사+주어+동사원형…?'의 어순이며 Yes/No로 대답할 수 있다.

A: Would you allow me to buy them?
B: Yes, I would. / No, I wouldn't.
Wouldn't you like to drink a glass of juice?
Can you help the stranger?
Can't she swim?

Activity 1

다음 제시된 의문문에 적절한 대답을 연결해보세요.

When did you finish your homework?　● 　　● Yes, I like riding a bicycle.

Can you print out some paper?　● 　　● No, I'm a high school student.

Are you a middle school student?　● 　　● I did my homework yesterday.

Don't you like riding a bicycle?　● 　　● Yes, I can print them.

Activity 2

다음 주어진 의문문 중 Yes/No로 대답할 수 있는것을 O, 대답할 수 없는 것을 X로 분류해보세요.

❶ Are they happy?

❷ What is your hobby?

❸ Where are you from?

❹ Would you do me a favor?

❺ Can you see the mountain?

❻ Who is your brother in the picture?

Exercise 1

알맞은 단어를 골라 문장을 완성하세요.

❶ **Who / What**   did you eat for lunch?

❷ **What / How**   can I get there?

❸ **Did / Were**   you watch the TV show yesterday?

❹ **Would / Did**   you allow me to use your computer?

❺ **Couldn't / Isn't**   she pretty?

Exercise 2

보기의 단어를 적절한 형태로 활용하여, 빈칸에 알맞은 단어를 쓰세요.

보기	Can	Who	Where	Did	Why

❶ _____ can we get some cheese?
우리는 어디에서 치즈를 얻을 수 있니?

❷ _____ you watch the movie?
그 영화 봤어?

❸ _____ are you so sad?
왜 그렇게 슬퍼하고 있어?

❹ _____ you lend your book?
너의 책을 빌려줄 수 있어?

❺ _____ is your best friend?
너의 가장 친한 친구가 누구야?

Sentence Completion

1. A: _____ are you so late?
   B: I'm late due to the traffic jam.

   (A) Who
   (B) How
   (C) Why
   (D) Where

2. A: _____ you remember this place?
   B: This was where we first met, wasn't it?

   (A) Why
   (B) Don't
   (C) Where
   (D) Doesn't

3. A: _____ they from South Africa?
   B: Yes, they are African.

   (A) Are
   (B) How
   (C) What
   (D) Where

4. A: _____ can we get the tickets?
   B: I saw a box office near the entrance.

   (A) Why
   (B) What
   (C) Don't
   (D) Where

5. A: _____ you give me some water?
   B: There is no water, but some milk.

   (A) Are
   (B) Why
   (C) What
   (D) Could

6 A: _____ are you doing here?

B: I am looking for a place to hide.

(A) Can

(B) Who

(C) Don't

(D) What

7 A: _____ you see my wallet?

B: No, I didn't see it.

(A) Are

(B) Did

(C) What

(D) Where

8 A: _____ does the sale end?

B: I heard it was until Friday.

(A) Why

(B) Who

(C) What

(D) When

9 A: _____ you go to school yesterday?

B: Yes, I forgot it was a holiday.

(A) Did

(B) Does

(C) When

(D) Could

10 A: _____ you like something to drink?

B: No, I'm fine, thank you.

(A) Can

(B) Does

(C) What

(D) Would

UNIT 3 의문문

1 graduate
졸업하다

2 allow
허락하다

3 legend
전설

4 dinner
저녁

5 answer
답

6 restaurant

식당, 레스토랑

restaurant

7 plan

계획

plan

8 stranger

낯선 사람

stranger

9 allow

허락하다

allow

10 wish

원하다, 바라다

wish

UNIT 3 의문문

Unit Review

배운 내용 스스로 정리해보기

❶ 의문사가 있는 의문문

의문사가 있는 의문문은 의문사 ❶ _____, ❷ _____, ❸ _____, ❹ _____, ❺ _____, ❻ _____, ❼ _____ 등을 사용한 문장으로 Yes/No로 대답 할 수 ❽ _____.

예시문장 써보기

① 의문사+be동사+주어…? ➜ _____

② 의문사+do[does/did]+주어+동사원형…?

➜ _____

❷ 의문사가 없는 의문문

의문사가 없는 의문문은 의문사를 사용하지 않은 문장으로 Yes/No로 대답할 수 ❶ _____.

예시문장 써보기

① be동사+주어…?'의 부정의문문

➜ _____

② Do[Does/Did]+주어+동사원형…?'의 긍정의문문

➜ _____

❸ 조동사 의문문

조동사 의문문은 ❶ _____ 의 어순이며 Yes/No로 대답할 수 ❷ _____.

예시문장 써보기

① 긍정의문문 ➜ _____

② 부정의문문 ➜ _____

UNIT 04

부가의문문

긍정문	부정 부가의문문	답 : 긍정이면 yes, 부정이면 no
부정문	긍정 부가의문문	

picnic	소풍	wear	입다
place	장소	expensive	비싼
visitor	방문자	abroad	해외에, 해외로
fresh	신선한	hospital	병원
prepare	준비하다	problem	문제

자신의 말에 대한 상대방의 확인이나 동의를 구하기 위해서 평서문 뒤에 덧붙이는 의문문.

❶ 앞 문장이 일반 동사인 경우

부가의문문의 동사는 앞 문장의 일반동사의 인칭과 시제에 따라 do[does, did]를 쓰며
부정의 부가의문문은 축약형을 사용한다.

긍정문	부정 부가의문문	대답
Jane wears an expensive dress,	doesn't she?	Yes, she does.
		No, she doesn't.
Peter went on a picnic last weekend,	didn't he?	Yes, he did.
		No, he didn't.
부정문	**긍정 부가의문문**	**대답**
Amy doesn't know the place,	does she?	Yes, she does.
		No, she doesn't.
They didn't prepare fresh vegetables,	did they?	Yes, they did.
		No, they didn't.

> **TIP** 부가의문문 대답
>
> • 긍정의 답이면 무조건 'Yes, 긍정문' 부정의 답이면 'No, 부정문'

❷ 앞 문장이 조동사인 경우

부가의문문의 동사는 앞 문장의 조동사를 그대로 쓰며 부정의 부가의문문은 축약형을 사용한다.

긍정문	부정 부가의문문	대답
Visitors can take a picture,	can't they?	Yes, they can.
		No, they can't.
Carl will go to the hospital,	won't he?	Yes, he will.
		No, he won't.
부정문	**긍정 부가의문문**	**대답**
She won't go abroad,	will she?	Yes, she will.
		No, she won't.
He wouldn't make a problem,	would he?	Yes, he would.
		No, he wouldn't.

❸ 앞 문장이 be 동사인 경우

부가의문문의 동사는 앞 문장의 be동사를 그대로 쓰며 부정의 부가의문문은 축약형을 사용한다.

긍정문	부정 부가의문문	대답
It is your bag,	isn't it?	Yes, it is.
		No, it isn't.
They are wise,	aren't they?	Yes, they are.
		No, they aren't.

부정문	긍정 부가의문문	대답
He wasn't at the station,	was he?	Yes, he was.
		No, he wasn't.
Tom isn't able to speak German,	is he?	Yes, he is.
		No, he isn't.

Activity 1

다음 제시된 문장에 적절한 부가의문문을 연결해보세요.

He is a tall guy, ●   ● doesn't she?

They can finish the work, ●   ● isn't he?

She has a younger sister, ●   ● does he?

He doesn't know her, ●   ● can't they?

Activity 2

보기에서 알맞은 부가의문문을 골라 쓰세요.

> **보기**   doesn't he   can't she   are you   did they

❶ He runs fast, _____ ?

❷ She can sing well, _____ ?

❸ You are not alone, _____ ?

❹ They didn't know each other, _____ ?

Exercise 1

알맞은 단어를 골라 문장을 완성하세요.

❶ He wears an expensive watch, **does he / doesn't he** ?

❷ She is a good teacher, **isn't she / doesn't she** ?

❸ We couldn't see the sunrise, **can we / could we** ?

❹ They won't go to a concert, **would they / will they** ?

❺ We didn't know how to get there, **did we / didn't we** ?

Exercise 2

보기의 단어를 적절한 형태로 활용하여, 빈칸에 알맞은 단어를 쓰세요.

| 보기 | won't   did   are   can't   made |

❶ She _____ some cookies, didn't she?
그녀는 몇몇 쿠키를 만들었어, 그렇지 않니?

❷ They _____ good friends, aren't they?
그들은 좋은 친구들이야, 그렇지 않니?

❸ He _____ run fast, can he?
그는 빠르게 달릴 수 없어, 그렇지?

❹ You _____ buy the same things, will you?
너는 같은 물건을 사지 않을 것이야, 그렇지?

❺ He _____ a good job, didn't he?
그는 멋진 일을 해냈어, 그렇지 않니?

Sentence Completion

1 A: Where is my hat?

   B: It was on the table, [   ] it?

   (A) was
   (B) wasn't
   (C) doesn't
   (D) wouldn't

4 A: You don't know the answer,

   [   ] you?

   B: Why don't we ask the teacher?

   (A) do
   (B) are
   (C) don't
   (D) aren't

2 A: How can we get there?

   B: We can go by bus, [   ] we?

   (A) are
   (B) can
   (C) can't
   (D) doesn't

5 A: We [   ] make some dishes
      for him, can't we?

   B: Ok, let's start cooking.

   (A) are
   (B) can
   (C) will
   (D) does

3 A: Where is he?

   B: He [   ] in the hospital, isn't he?

   (A) is
   (B) can
   (C) will
   (D) does

6 A: We didn't have enough money,

_____ we?

B: We had a hard time during the trip.

(A) are

(B) did

(C) can

(D) does

9 A: The tour guide was so kind,

_____ she?

B: Yes, I liked her.

(A) was

(B) does

(C) wasn't

(D) doesn't

7 A: They won't go to the museum,

_____ they?

B: No, they don't have enough time.

(A) will

(B) won't

(C) would

(D) wouldn't

10 A: It contains a lot of vitamins,

_____ it?

B: Yes, I checked the ingredients.

(A) is

(B) isn't

(C) does

(D) doesn't

8 A: We can't use a calculator in the math

exam, _____ we?

B: No, we can't use it.

(A) do

(B) can

(C) don't

(D) can't

1 **picnic**
소풍

picnic

2 **place**
장소

place

3 **visitor**
방문자

visitor

4 **fresh**
신선한

fresh

5 **prepare**
준비하다

prepare

6 wear
입다

wear

7 expensive
비싼

expensive

8 abroad
해외에, 해외로

abroad

9 hospital
병원

hospital

10 problem
문제

problem

Unit Review

배운 내용 스스로 정리해보기

❶ 앞 문장이 일반동사인 경우

부가의문문의 동사는 앞 문장의 일반동사의 인칭과 시제에 따라 ❶   (을)를 쓰며
부정의 부가의문문은 ❷   형을 사용한다.

예시문장 써보기

① 긍정문 ➜ _____

② 부정문 ➜ _____

❷ 앞 문장이 조동사인 경우

부가의문문의 동사는 앞 문장의 ❶   (을)를 그대로 쓰며 부정의 부가의문문은
❷   형을 사용한다.

예시문장 써보기

① 긍정문 ➜ _____

② 부정문 ➜ _____

❸ 앞 문장이 be동사인 경우

부가의문문의 동사는 앞 문장의 ❶   (을)를 그대로 쓰며 부정의 부가의문문은
❷   의 형을 사용한다.

예시문장 써보기

① 긍정문 ➜ _____

② 부정문 ➜ _____

TOSEL 실전문제 ❻

SECTION II. Reading and Writing

PART A. Sentence Completion

DIRECTIONS: For questions 1 to 20, fill in the blanks to complete the sentences. Choose the option that BEST completes each blank.

지시 사항: 1번부터 20번까지는 빈칸을 알맞게 채워 대화를 완성하는 문제입니다. 가장 알맞은 답을 고르세요.

1. A: Where is he?
   B: He _____ in the middle of the line.

   (A) is

   (B) are

   (C) wait

   (D) does

2. A: She doesn't like to eat salad, _____ she?
   B: Yes, she likes to eat salad.

   (A) is

   (B) do

   (C) isn't

   (D) does

3. A: _____ off the air conditioner.
   B: Ok, it's too cold here.

   (A) Turn

   (B) Turns

   (C) Turned

   (D) Turning

4. A: _____ is your birthday?
   B: It's in January.

   (A) Why

   (B) What

   (C) When

   (D) Where

5. A: Don't let me _____ a new dress.
   B: Ok, give me your credit card.

   (A) buy

   (B) buys

   (C) bought

   (D) buying

6. A: The ball is yours, _____ it?
    B: No, it's not mine.

    (A) is

    (B) does

    (C) isn't

    (D) doesn't

9. A: He will go to another company, _____ he?

    B: Yes, I heard about it.

    (A) is

    (B) will

    (C) isn't

    (D) won't

7. A: I'm so hungry.
    B: She _____ tasty cookies.

    (A) bring

    (B) brings

    (C) bringing

    (D) brought

10. A: The criminal _____ on the court.
    B: He committed a lot of crimes.

    (A) appear

    (B) appeared

    (C) to appear

    (D) appearing

8. A: _____ you like eating salad?
    B: Yes, I love it.

    (A) What

    (B) Can

    (C) Were

    (D) Don't

11. A: _____ is your roommate?
    B: My roommate is Amy, and she is neat and tidy.

    (A) Do

    (B) Who

    (C) What

    (D) When

12. A: _____ your desk before you study.
    B: There are a lot of books on the desk.

    (A) Clean

    (B) Cleans

    (C) Cleaned

    (D) Cleaning

13. A: Our teacher is so _____ to us.
    B: I think so too.

    (A) kind

    (B) kindly

    (C) kinding

    (D) kindness

14. A: That isn't your car, _____?
    B: No, my car is black.

    (A) is it

    (B) isn't it

    (C) does it

    (D) aren't they

15. A: _____ I ask you a question?
    B: Sure, you can ask anything.

    (A) Can

    (B) Who

    (C) What

    (D) Don't

16. A: Your sisters are students, _____?
    B: Yes, they will graduate soon.

    (A) isn't it

    (B) was it

    (C) were they

    (D) aren't they

17. A: _____ you please be quiet?
    B: I'm sorry. We will move the seat.

    (A) Do

    (B) Did

    (C) Are

    (D) Can

18. A: _____ are you so happy?
    B: Because I won the first prize.

    (A) Why

    (B) Who

    (C) Which

    (D) Where

19. A: _____ more loudly so everyone can hear.
    B: Can I have a microphone instead?

    (A) Speak

    (B) Spoke

    (C) Speaks

    (D) Speaking

20. A: What is that in the bag?
    B: I _____ new shoes.

    (A) to buy

    (B) buying

    (C) bought

    (D) buy for

Answers

Short Answers

UNIT 1 p.23
Activity

1. quickly   2. easily   3. truly   4. hard

1. fortunately   2. young   3. small   4. loudly   5. wholly

Exercise 1 p.25

1. easily   2. fast   3. huge   4. so strong   5. something small

Exercise 2

1. early   2. busy   3. correctly   4. quickly   5. hard

Sentence Completion p.26

1. (B)   2. (D)   3. (C)   4. (C)   5. (B)   6. (A)   7. (A)   8. (B)   9. (B)   10. (B)

Unit Review p.30

1. ❶ ➡ He completely forgot the schedule.   ❷ ➡ She always works hard.

2. ❶ 명사   ❷ 대명사   ❸ 주어   ❹ 형용사
   ❺ 동사   ❻ 부사   ❼ 문장 전체

❶ ➡ The puppy has short legs.   ❷ ➡ I am so grateful.

❸ ➡ I looked closely at the screen.

UNIT 2 p.33
Activity

1. books, dolls   2. money, coffee

1. friends - many   2. errors - a few   3. coffee - much   4. money - little   5. newspapers - many

Exercise 1 p.35

1. many   2. much   3. bookstores   4. a few   5. lots of

Exercise 2

1. a great deal of (much)   2. many   3. lots of   4. a few   5. much

Sentence Completion p.36

1. (B)   2. (C)   3. (A)   4. (B)   5. (D)   6. (D)   7. (C)   8. (D)   9. (A)   10. (A)

Unit Review p.40

1. ❶ many   ❷ much
   ❶ ➡ There are many books on her bookshelf.   ❷ ➡ He found much information about AI.

2. ❶ 셀 수 있는   ❷ 셀 수 없는   ❸ 명사
   ❶ ➡ A lot of people hope their bright future.   ❷ ➡ There is a lot of love in your heart.

3. ❶ ➡ We have a great number of invitations.   ❷ ➡ We need a great deal of sugar.

UNIT 3 p.43
Activity

1. 항상   2. 가끔   3. 결코 ~ 않다   4. 보통   5. 좀처럼 ~ 않다

1. always, often, hardly, never, seldom

Exercise 1 p.45

1. always got up   2. usually skips   3. is often   4. can hardly   5. is rarely

Exercise 2

1. never   2. always   3. usually   4. sometimes   5. often

Sentence Completion p.46

1. (A)   2. (A)   3. (B)   4. (B)   5. (D)   6. (D)   7. (B)   8. (D)   9. (A)   10. (C)

Unit Review p.50

1. ❶ always   ❷ usually   ❸ often
   ❹ sometimes   ❺ seldom [rarely, hardly]   ❻ never
   ❶ ➡ I always review the book.   ❷ ➡ Cathy usually goes jogging.
   ❸ ➡ Andy is often late for school.

2. ❶ be동사   ❷ 조동사   ❸ 일반동사
   ❶ ➡ She is always wise.   ❷ ➡ I can hardly[seldom, rarely] swim well.
   ❸ ➡ He sometimes goes to the park.

UNIT 4 p.53
Activity

1. better   2. worst   3. hottest
4. larger   5. largest   6. more difficult

1. more expensive   2. green   3. heaviest
4. older   5. yellow   6. black, most expensive

Exercise 1 p.55

1. taller   2. faster   3. biggest   4. important   5. most

Exercise 2

1. interesting   2. higher   3. wiser   4. most   5. more

Sentence Completion p.56

1. (C)   2. (B)   3. (B)   4. (A)   5. (C)   6. (D)   7. (C)   8. (C)   9. (D)   10. (D)

Unit Review p.60	✏ 1. ❶ 형용사/부사의 원급 + -er	❷ more + 원급							
	❶ ➡ He is taller than me.	❷ ➡ Kate is more generous than Sora.							
	✏ 2. ❶ 형용사/부사의 원급 + -est	❷ most + 원급							
	❶ ➡ Winter is the coldest season in Korea.	❷ ➡ She is the most famous author in the world.							
TOSEL 실전문제 4	1. (C) 2. (D) 3. (C) 4. (D) 5. (C) 6. (D) 7. (D) 8. (D) 9. (A) 10. (B)								
	11. (A) 12. (B) 13. (A) 14. (A) 15. (C) 16. (A) 17. (C) 18. (C) 19. (B) 20. (D)								

CHAPTER 5 p.66

UNIT 1 p.69	✏ 1. ...고, ... 와	2. 또는, 혹은	3. ...지만, ...(으)나		
▶ Activity	✏ 1. man and woman	2. yes or no	3. expensive but valuable		
▶ Exercise 1 p.71	✏ 1. and	2. but	3. but	4. and	5. or
▶ Exercise 2	✏ 1. or	2. and	3. but	4. and	5. or
▶ Sentence Completion p.72	✏ 1. (D) 2. (A) 3. (D) 4. (A) 5. (B) 6. (C) 7. (A) 8. (B) 9. (D) 10. (A)				
▶ Unit Review p.76	✏ 1. ❶ 비슷한				
	❶ ➡ I chose a red one and a blue one.	❷ ➡ He is tired and sleepy.			
	✏ 2. ❶ 대조되는				
	❶ ➡ English is difficult but interesting.	❷ ➡ Daisy studied slowly but honestly.			
	✏ 3. ❶ 선택				
	❶ ➡ Would you like pork or beef?	❷ ➡ Is the news true or false?			
UNIT 2 p.79	✏ 1. ...(하기) 전에	2. ...(한) 이후에	3. 그래서, 그러므로	4. ...(할) 때	5. ... 때문에
▶ Activity	✏ 1. because, before, when, but, after				
▶ Exercise 1 p.81	✏ 1. After	2. when	3. or	4. so	5. Because
▶ Exercise 2	✏ 1. because	2. but	3. or	4. Before	5. After
▶ Sentence Completion p.82	✏ 1. (C) 2. (A) 3. (D) 4. (C) 5. (C) 6. (C) 7. (B) 8. (A) 9. (A) 10. (B)				
▶ Unit Review p.86	✏ 1. ❶ 문법적 기능이 같은	❶ ➡ The dog is on the cushion and the cat is on the drawer.			
	❷ ➡ I hate insects but she likes them.	❸ ➡ My friend came home yesterday, so I was happy.			
	✏ 2. ❶ 종속절 ❷ 주절	❶ ➡ I was ten years old when I first learned English.			
	❷ ➡ Please knock before you open the door.	❸ ➡ Because I admire my father, I always listen to him.			
UNIT 3 p.89	✏ 1. ...동안(시간의 길이)	2. 위쪽에	3. ...까지 (계속)	4. 아래에	5. ...동안(특정 기간)
▶ Activity	✏ 1. on - Wednesday	2. in - the morning	3. at - 9 o'clock	4. during - summer vacation	5. for - one hour
▶ Exercise 1 p.91	✏ 1. during	2. at	3. before	4. above	5. by
▶ Exercise 2	✏ 1. on	2. by	3. above	4. For	5. under
▶ Sentence Completion p.92	✏ 1. (D) 2. (C) 3. (B) 4. (B) 5. (B) 6. (A) 7. (D) 8. (B) 9. (C) 10. (D)				
▶ Unit Review p.96	✏ 1. ❶ ➡ We made a huge snowman in winter.	❷ ➡ I usually get up at six o'clock.			
	❸ ➡ Let's meet on Wednesday.	❹ ➡ I wrote an essay for two hours.			
	✏ 2. ❶ ➡ We had a party in the garden.	❷ ➡ He arrived at the station.			
	❸ ➡ Your comb is on the floor.	❹ ➡ The plane is flying over the mountain.			
UNIT 4 p.99	✏ 1. ...없이	2. ...때문에, ...(으)로 인하여	3. ...에 대한	4. ...에 의하여, ...(으)로	5. ...(으)로 만들어지다
▶ Activity	✏ 1. by go	2. Due to it is heavy	3. made about soil	4. book at history	5. upset by she fails to the exam
▶ Exercise 1 p.101	✏ 1. due to	2. by	3. about	4. on	5. of
▶ Exercise 2	✏ 1. by	2. without	3. Due to	4. from	5. of
▶ Sentence Completion p.102	✏ 1. (B) 2. (A) 3. (A) 4. (A) 5. (D) 6. (D) 7. (D) 8. (D) 9. (D) 10. (A)				
▶ Unit Review p.106	✏ 1. ❶ ➡ I painted the wall with a brush.	❷ ➡ He practiced a presentation without an audience.			
	❸ ➡ My mother goes to work by her car.	❹ ➡ Wine is made from grapes.			
	❺ ➡ The house is made of wood.	❻ ➡ This result is due to the team's efforts.			
	❼ ➡ This is a book about language.				
TOSEL 실전문제 5	1. (C) 2. (C) 3. (D) 4. (B) 5. (A) 6. (D) 7. (D) 8. (B) 9. (C) 10. (A)				
	11. (D) 12. (C) 13. (B) 14. (C) 15. (A) 16. (D) 17. (C) 18. (C) 19. (B) 20. (D)				

UNIT 1 p.115

Activity

1. They came late.   2. He is my teacher.   3. I like you.

1. ① The girl lives in Seoul.   ② The girl is a student.
    ③ The girl made some cookies.

2. ① The puppy lives with me.   ② The puppy is big.
    ③ My grandpa bought a puppy.

3. ① People cried.   ② The people are noisy.
    ③ People are reading books.

Exercise 1 p.117

1. 3형식   2. 2형식   3. 1형식   4. 2형식   5. 3형식

Exercise 2

1. O - teaches   □ - difficult science topics   2. O - fell   △ - asleep   3. O - is   △ - empty
4. O - arrived   5. O - was   △ - beautiful

Sentence Completion p.118

1. (B)   2. (A)   3. (D)   4. (D)   5. (C)   6. (C)   7. (B)   8. (B)   9. (B)   10. (D)

Unit Review p.122

1. ① 주어 + 완전자동사 (S + V)   ① ➡ The book sells well.

2. ① 주어 + 불완전자동사 + 주격보어 (S + V + S.C.)   ① ➡ Kristin became a judge.

3. ① 주어 + 타동사 + 목적어(S + V + O)   ① ➡ We bought a bicycle for your present.

UNIT 2 p.125

Activity

1. Wash your hands.   2. Don't worry about that.   3. Be careful.   4. Close the window.

1. Wash   2. worry   3. Give   4. Turn off

Exercise 1 p.127

1. myself   2. Don't   3. Tell   4. jump   5. worry

Exercise 2

1. alone   2. Give   3. go   4. let   5. Catch

Sentence Completion p.128

1. (A)   2. (A)   3. (B)   4. (C)   5. (A)   6. (A)   7. (B)   8. (A)   9. (C)   10. (C)

Unit Review p.132

1. ① 상대방   ② 동사원형   ③ Don't +동사원형…   ④ Never +동사원형…
    ① ➡ Pass me the ball.   ② ➡ Don't[Never] rush.

2. ① 1인칭   ② 3인칭   ③ Let + 목적어 + 동사원형…   ④ Don't let + 목적어 + 동사원형…
    ① ➡ Let him reply the email.   ② ➡ Don't let them speak loudly at night.

UNIT 3 p.135

Activity

1. I did my homework yesterday.   2. Yes, I can print them.
3. No, I'm a high school student.   4. Yes, I like riding a bicycle.

(O) 1, 4, 5   (X) 2, 3, 6

Exercise 1 p.137

1. What   2. How   3. Did   4. Would   5. Isn't

Exercise 2

1. Where   2. Did   3. Why   4. Can   5. Who

Sentence Completion p.138

1. (C)   2. (B)   3. (A)   4. (D)   5. (D)   6. (D)   7. (B)   8. (D)   9. (A)   10. (D)

Unit Review p.142

1. ① Who ② When ③ Where ④ What ⑤ Why ⑥ Which ⑦ How ⑧ 없다
    ① ➡ When is your birthday?   ② ➡ Where did you buy it?

2. ① 있다   ① ➡ Isn't she pretty?   ② ➡ Does she speak English?

3. ① 조동사 +주어 +동사원형…?   ② 있다
    ① ➡ Can you help me?   ② ➡ Don't you have homework to do?

UNIT 4 p.145

Activity

1. isn't he?   2. can't they?   3. doesn't she?   4. does he?

1. doesn't he   2. can't she   3. are you   4. did they

Exercise 1 p.147

1. doesn't he   2. isn't she   3. could we   4. will they   5. did we

Exercise 2

1. made   2. are   3. can't   4. won't   5. did

Sentence Completion p.148

1. (B)   2. (C)   3. (A)   4. (A)   5. (B)   6. (B)   7. (A)   8. (B)   9. (C)   10. (D)

Unit Review p.152

1. ① do [does, did]   ② 축약
    ① ➡ Helen exercises regularly, doesn't she?   ② ➡ They didn't attend the class, did they?

2. ① 조동사   ② 축약
    ① ➡ You will help me, won't you?   ② ➡ She wouldn't argue with him, would she?

3. ① be동사   ② 축약
    ① ➡ He is your older brother, isn't he?   ② ➡ Mia wasn't at the party, was she?

TOSEL 실전문제 6

1. (A)   2. (D)   3. (A)   4. (C)   5. (A)   6. (C)   7. (B)   8. (D)   9. (D)   10. (B)
11. (B)   12. (A)   13. (A)   14. (A)   15. (A)   16. (D)   17. (D)   18. (A)   19. (A)   20. (C)

MEMO